2,200 AI PROMPTS

The Secret Box to Unlock Unlimited Creativity

KOUADIO KONAN JOEL

Cover design by: Art Painter
Library of Congress Control Number: 2018675309
Printed in the United States of America

CONTENTS

Category

2,200 AI Prompts

The Secret Box to Unlock Unlimited Creativity

BOOK PLAN

Artificial intelligence is taking over many fields, revolutionizing various industries through automation, data analytics, and machine learning. Here is a list of the major areas of application of AI:

1. Content Creation and Media

- Text Generation (ChatGPT, Jasper AI)
- Image and video creation (DALL·E, Runway ML)
- Speech synthesis and deepfakes
- Video and audio editing automation
- AI-assisted journalism

2. Computer Science and Software Development

- Code generation (GitHub Copilot, Codeium)
- Automatic error detection and correction
- Cybersecurity and intrusion detection
- Software Test Automation
- Optimization of algorithms and systems

3. Medicine and Health

- AI-assisted diagnosis (radiology, dermatology, cardiology)
- Drug development and biomedical research
- Medical image analysis
- Assisting surgeons through robotics

- Patient monitoring and personalized medicine

4. Finance and Economics

- Analysis and prediction of financial markets
- Banking Fraud Detection
- Automation of investment advice (robo-advisors)
- Credit Scoring and Risk Management
- Optimization of financial management

5. Education and Training

- Virtual Tutors and Learning Assistants
- Creation of interactive and personalized online courses
- Analysis of student performance
- Automatic generation of quizzes and educational materials
- Automatic translation and transcription

6. Marketing and E-Commerce

- Personalization of product recommendations
- Consumer Behavior Analysis
- Chatbots and virtual assistants for customer service
- Creation of targeted and optimized advertisements
- Automatic generation of product descriptions

7. Industry and Automation

- Predictive maintenance of equipment
- Supply chain optimization
- Automated quality control
- Industrial robotics
- Optimized production planning

8. Transport and Mobility

- Autonomous vehicles (Tesla, Waymo)
- Traffic optimization and transport management
- Intelligent navigation systems
- Predictive analysis of road incidents
- Automation of logistics and deliveries

9. Agriculture and Environment

- Crop monitoring and disease detection
- Optimization of irrigation and natural resources
- Weather forecasting
- Soil analysis and yield optimization
- Waste management and automated sorting

10. Law and Security

- Automatic analysis of contracts and legal documents
- Detection of fraud and regulatory violations
- Surveillance and facial recognition
- Crime prediction and risk management

- Assistance with judicial decision-making

11. Art and Entertainment

- AI-generated music (AIVA, OpenAI Jukebox)
- Scenario creation and automated storytelling
- Optimized animation and special effects
- Video games with adaptive AI
- Interactive experiences and augmented realities

INTRODUCTION

Artificial Intelligence (AI) is revolutionizing the way we create, innovate, and interact with the digital world. Whether you're an entrepreneur, content creator, marketer, writer, designer, or simply curious about the endless possibilities of AI, this book is for you.

Welcome to **"2,200 AI Prompts: The Secret Box to Unlock Unlimited Creativity ,"** a must-read guide that offers you **an exclusive collection of prompts** designed to harness the power of AI in every field. With these prompts, you'll be able to generate unique content, refine your ideas, automate tasks, and maximize your productivity like never before.

Why this book?

In a world where AI is becoming an essential tool for creation and innovation, **knowing how to formulate effective prompts is a key skill** . A good prompt can transform a simple query into a work of art, a captivating text, a powerful marketing strategy or even a scientific breakthrough. **The art of prompt engineering** will allow you to obtain optimal results and fully exploit the capabilities of artificial intelligences like ChatGPT, MidJourney, DALL·E, and many others.

What you will discover

This book is divided into several categories to cover **all** the areas where AI can be used :

☐ **Content and media creation** (blogs, videos, social networks, podcasts)

☐ **Marketing and advertising** (SEO, copywriting, branding, digital advertising)

☐ **Business and entrepreneurship** (strategies, automation, innovation)

☐ **Design and creativity** (illustrations, logos, UI/UX, graphics)

☐ **Personal development and productivity** (mindset, organization, efficiency)

☐ **Science, technology and education** (research, analysis, learning)

☐ **And much more!**

How to use this book?

This book is designed as **a practical and interactive tool** . You can:

☐ **Find instant ideas** for your creative and professional projects

☐ **Customize prompts** to your specific needs

☐ **Experimenting with AI** to explore new approaches and concepts

☐ **Optimize your results** by adjusting suggestions for even more precise and powerful outputs

The future is in your hands

Whether you want **to write a book, create viral content, optimize your business or simply explore the infinite capabilities of AI** , this book will give you **the keys to unleash your creative potential** .

So, ready to unlock unlimited creativity? ☐☐

Happy exploring and may AI boost your imagination!

CHAPTER 1. CONTENT CREATION AND MEDIA

AI and the Content Creation and Media Revolution

Artificial intelligence is radically transforming the world of content creation and media. Whether it's **writing articles, generating impactful visuals, creating videos or optimizing production processes** , AI offers powerful tools that push the boundaries of creativity. This revolution does not replace humans, but allows them to **gain in efficiency, precision and originality** .

In this development, we will explore **the main applications of AI in content and media creation** , illustrated by concrete examples and use cases.

1. Text generation: AI as a writing assistant

Tools like **ChatGPT, Jasper AI or Copy.ai** allow you to **automatically write articles, product descriptions, video scripts and marketing content** . These tools are particularly useful for:

- **Bloggers and journalists** : Writing articles,

generating summaries and analyzing trends.

- **Marketers** : Creating slogans, promotional emails and advertising hooks.
- **Screenwriters and writers** : Generation of synopses, dialogues and scenarios.

Example:
An entrepreneur launching a new product can use **Jasper AI** to generate a compelling description and optimize its SEO in minutes.

2. Image and video creation: AI as a graphics studio

AI is also revolutionizing **the creation of visuals and animations** with tools like **DALL·E, Runway ML or MidJourney** . These technologies make it possible to **create ultra-realistic images and videos** from simple text descriptions.

- **For designers and artists** : Generate illustrations and posters in seconds.
- **For brands and influencers** : Creation of unique and attractive marketing visuals.
- **For cinema and advertising** : Production of special effects and innovative editing.

Example:
A graphic designer can use **DALL·E** to generate a visual concept to present to their client before even starting to draw.

3. Speech synthesis and deepfakes: voices and faces that are more real than life

AI now makes it possible to **generate realistic voices and manipulate videos** with technologies such as **Descript, ElevenLabs or DeepFaceLab** . These advances have major applications in:

- **Podcasting and narration** : Creating synthetic voices for audiobooks and videos.
- **Dubbing and machine translation** : Adapting content into multiple languages without losing authenticity.
- **Special effects and video retouching** : Creation of deepfakes and digital avatars for entertainment.

Example:
A company can use **ElevenLabs** to produce multilingual versions of its promotional videos without hiring voice actors.

4. Automation of video and audio editing: a considerable time saving

Editing a video or podcast can be time-consuming, but tools like **Runway ML, Adobe Sensei, and Descript** help automate **editing, removing noise, and optimizing transitions** .

- **For YouTubers** : Fast editing and automatic

synchronization of images and sound.

- **For podcasters** : Remove silence and improve audio quality with one click.
- **For production agencies** : Acceleration of the post-production process.

Example:
A content creator can use **Runway ML** to edit a YouTube video without any technical editing knowledge.

5. AI-assisted journalism: faster access to information

AI is also an **ally of journalism** , allowing:

- **Analyze and summarize large amounts of information** .
- **Detect trends and generate automated reports** .
- **Checking facts and fighting fake news** with AI.

Example:
A writer can use **ChatGPT** to get an instant summary of a 100-page report and save valuable time.

Conclusion: AI, a lever of innovation for content creation

AI doesn't replace human creativity, but it amplifies it. With these tools, **content creators can produce faster,**

explore new styles, and improve their impact . Whether writing, designing, editing, or analyzing, AI opens up a **world of opportunities** in media and communications.

By leveraging these prompts and testing these tools, everyone can **reinvent the way they create and share content** . AI is no longer just a gadget, it is a true **creative partner** for the future of digital production.

Here are 200 prompts divided into several categories for content creation and media.

1. Creating Text and Articles (20 prompts)

1. Write an article on the impact of AI in digital marketing.
2. Write a practical guide to SEO in 2025.
3. Write an article about e-commerce trends.
4. Develop a text on the mistakes to avoid in entrepreneurship.
5. Make a top 10 of the most influential books for entrepreneurs.
6. Write a comparative article between freelancing and salaried employment.
7. Offers an analysis of the best growth hacking

strategies.

8. Write a FAQ about creating online content.
9. Write a guide on personal branding on LinkedIn.
10. Explains how to succeed in storytelling in copywriting.
11. Write an article about the best platforms for selling online courses.
12. Write a productivity guide for content creators.
13. Explains the importance of color psychology in marketing.
14. Write an article about the future of influencers in the age of AI.
15. Compare content creation tools (Canva, ChatGPT, etc.).
16. Offers a tutorial for creating a content strategy in 5 steps.
17. Write an article about monetizing a blog in 2025.
18. Write a guide on creating and selling ebooks.
19. Analyzes common mistakes of beginning entrepreneurs.
20. Offers a checklist for a successful digital marketing campaign.

2. Storytelling and Scenarios (20 prompts)

21. Imagine the story of an entrepreneur who lost everything before succeeding.

22. Describe the opening scene of a psychological thriller.

23. Write an interior monologue of a character before a big event.

24. Imagine an advertisement with an emotional storytelling for a chocolate brand.

25. Create a scary urban legend for an imaginary city.

26. Write a humorous anecdote about a professional failure.

27. Describe a movie scene where a robot becomes human.

28. Imagine an inspiring story about perseverance.

29. Write a modern tale with a moral about success.

30. Creates a dramatic scene between a father and son in disagreement.

31. Imagine a dialogue between two competitors in a crucial negotiation.

32. Write a humorous ad script for a tech startup.

33. Describe a long-distance love scene in the age of new technologies.

34. Imagine a story where an influencer

discovers a life-changing secret.

35. Write a YouTube video script about the most inspiring entrepreneurs.

36. Developing a mini-series on the daily life of a content creator.

37. Imagine a 30-second commercial about a revolutionary product.

38. Write a scene where an entrepreneur has to make a crucial choice.

39. Create a fictional biography of a self-made millionaire.

40. Imagine a short film scenario on the impact of social networks.

3. Social Media Content Creation (20 prompts)

41. Write a Twitter thread about the best digital marketing strategies.

42. Offers a series of Instagram posts about productivity.

43. Come up with an engaging Instagram caption for a travel photo.

44. Write a LinkedIn post about lessons from entrepreneurial failure.

45. Create a humorous TikTok script about working from home.

46. Offers an Instagram Reel video on business

tips.

47. Write a Facebook post about motivation and discipline.

48. Create a series of tweets about freelancing trends.

49. Imagine a LinkedIn post about networking and professional relationships.

50. Write a powerful intro for a YouTube video.

51. Create an Instagram carousel about content creation mistakes.

52. Write a powerful punchline for a motivational post.

53. Imagine an educational TikTok on soft skills.

54. Suggest 5 post ideas for a Facebook business page.

55. Create an engaging video to announce a product launch.

56. Write a viral caption for a humorous video.

57. Imagine a viral video concept about personal development.

58. Proposes a content strategy for a cosmetics brand.

59. Write a Facebook video script about mistakes beginner entrepreneurs make.

60. Write a LinkedIn post about the books that changed your business outlook.

4. AI Image and Visual Creation (20 prompts)

61. Generates a futuristic cyberpunk skyline image.
62. Create a prompt for Midjourney on a minimalist logo.
63. Imagine a fantasy scene with an AI dragon.
64. Describe a realistic post-apocalyptic landscape.
65. Generate a visual for an innovative electric car concept.
66. Create a cover illustration for a science fiction book.
67. Describe a realistic AI avatar for a digital entrepreneur.
68. Suggest a poster design for a tech festival.
69. Imagine a prompt to generate a modern business card.
70. Create a visual inspired by cyberpunk movies.
71. Generates an illustration of a medieval village under the snow.
72. Describe a video game character in precise detail.
73. Imagine a minimalist and futuristic tattoo design.
74. Offers an inspiring poster for an

entrepreneur's office.

75. Describe a humanoid AI in a dystopian universe.

76. Create an image for an ecological awareness campaign.

77. Imagine an advertising visual for an innovative startup.

78. Describe a logo for a wellness and meditation brand.

79. Create an 80s inspired movie poster.

80. Offers a prompt for a modern fairy tale illustration.81-100.

5. Copywriting and Advertising (20 prompts)

81. Write a catchy slogan for a tech startup.

82. Create an advertising text for an organic cosmetics brand.

83. Write an ad script for a productivity app.

84. Imagine a hook for a product launch campaign.

85. Write a marketing email for a limited special offer.

86. Write a Facebook ad for an online course.

87. Create a LinkedIn post to promote a coaching service.

88. Provide an engaging product description

for an online store.

89. Write a compelling sales page for an ebook.

90. Write a Google Ads ad for a freelancing service.

91. Imagine a poster ad for an energy drink.

92. Write a humorous advertising campaign for a clothing brand.

93. Create a series of punchlines for a streetwear brand.

94. Write a video ad script for a wellness brand.

95. Provides storytelling for an inspiring advertisement.

96. Write a follow-up email after an abandoned cart on an e-commerce site.

97. Create an engaging promotional Instagram post.

98. Imagine an advertisement for a B2B SaaS software.

99. Write an optimized YouTube description for a promotional video.

100.   Come up with an original concept for a TikTok ad.

6. Podcasts and Videos (20 prompts)

101.   Imagine the concept of a podcast on digital entrepreneurship.

102.   Write a powerful introduction

for a podcast episode.

103.   Create an outline for a YouTube video on the secrets of financial success.

104.   Offers a guest list for a podcast on innovation.

105.   Write a motivational video script for YouTube.

106.   Imagine a fictional interview with a famous entrepreneur.

107.   Creates a short podcast format about productivity.

108.   Write a teaser for a video series on personal growth.

109.   Proposes an original concept for an online talk show.

110.   Write an engaging call to action for a promotional video.

111.   Develop an educational YouTube channel idea.

112.   Imagine a vlog about a typical day of a digital entrepreneur.

113.   Write a script for a video explaining a current trend.

114.   Offers a concept of Instagram Reels mini-series on business.

115.   Write a storytelling script for a viral video.

116.   Imagine a video about common

mistakes in digital marketing.

117. Create a trailer for a documentary about artificial intelligence.

118. Write an engaging intro for an educational TikTok video.

119. Suggest a debate idea to host in a business podcast.

120. Write an ASMR video script about relaxation and concentration.

7. Creative Writing (20 prompts)

121. Imagine a poem inspired by the digital age.

122. Write a short story about the future of work.

123. Write a haiku about technological innovation.

124. Imagine a modern fable with an entrepreneurial moral.

125. Write a fictional letter from a billionaire to his younger self.

126. Write an introspective monologue from a content creator in crisis.

127. Imagine a conversation between two AIs in a dystopian future.

128. Write a text inspired by the minimalist movement.

129.   Create a story based on an initiatory journey into the business world.

130.   Write a dialogue between a mentor and his student about success.

131.   Imagine a dramatic scene about an ethical dilemma in artificial intelligence.

132.   Write a fictitious cover letter for a job of the future.

133.   Describe a utopia where AI coexists perfectly with humanity.

134.   Write a breakup letter between an entrepreneur and his first failed project.

135.   Imagine a mythological legend about the birth of innovation.

136.   Develops a science fiction text about an extraterrestrial start-up.

137.   Write a motivational speech from a fictional leader.

138.   Imagine a movie scene inspired by a major entrepreneurial failure.

139.   Write a list of advice in the form of modern proverbs.

140.   Write a slam on the challenges of entrepreneurship.

8. Newsletters and Emails (20 prompts)

141. Write an engaging welcome email for an online program.

142. Offers a weekly newsletter format on digital business.

143. Write a loyalty email for an e-commerce store.

144. Write a promotional email for a free webinar.

145. Imagine a newsletter with an inspiring story about a successful entrepreneur.

146. Create an email sequence to sell an online course.

147. Write an apology email after a late delivery.

148. Offers a prospecting email template for freelancers.

149. Write a re-engagement email for inactive subscribers.

150. Write an informative email about a product update.

151. Imagine a humorous email for a special Black Friday offer.

152. Write an inspiring newsletter about perseverance and success.

153. Create an invitation email to a virtual conference.

154. Provides a script for a

networking email after an event.

155.   Write a follow-up email for a hot B2B lead.

156.   Imagine a newsletter on digital marketing trends.

157.   Write a launch email for a new service.

158.   Offer an upsell email for an existing customer.

159.   Writes an educational newsletter on personal investing.

160.   Create an engaging email to announce an exclusive collaboration.

9. Finance and Business (20 prompts)

161.   Write an article about financial mistakes young entrepreneurs make.

162.   Offers a Twitter thread on investment strategies.

163.   Write a LinkedIn post about managing personal finances.

164.   Imagine a series of videos on finance for beginners.

165.   Write a guide on investing in cryptocurrencies.

166.   Offers an Instagram post about lessons from a millionaire entrepreneur.

167. Create an interactive quiz on the basics of investing.

168. Write a case study about a company that revolutionized its market.

169. Offers an article on time and money management.

170. Write a motivational post about financial independence.

171. Create a Twitter thread about profitable businesses in 2025.

172. Write a guide on passive income sources.

173. Offers an educational video on common financial mistakes.

174. Write a Facebook post about the psychology of money.

175. Imagine a podcast about personal finance and entrepreneurship.

176. Write a Twitter thread about managing debt intelligently.

177. Write an article on the most profitable business models.

178. Create an Instagram post about the golden rules of wealth.

179. Write a guide on financial management for freelancers.

180. Offers video content on must-read books in finance.

10. Personal Development and Motivation (20 prompts)

181. Write an article about the habits of successful entrepreneurs.

182. Write a Twitter thread about stress management and productivity.

183. Imagine a YouTube video about the best morning routines.

184. Create an Instagram post about the most inspiring quotes.

185. Write a podcast script about resilience in the face of failure.

186. Offers a 30-day challenge to improve personal discipline.

187. Write a motivating email for a personal development newsletter.

188. Write an article about visualization and goal achievement.

189. Imagine a LinkedIn post about time management and success.

190. Create an e-book concept on extreme productivity.

191. Writes a weekly newsletter on the mindset of leaders.

192. Offers a series of TikTok videos on the principles of success.

193.   Write a Facebook post about limiting beliefs and how to overcome them.

194.   Write a powerful introduction for a motivational seminar.

195.   Imagine a storytelling scenario about personal transformation.

196.   Create an interactive quiz on the type of mindset you need to adopt to succeed.

197.   Write an article about the importance of emotional intelligence.

198.   Offers an Instagram feed on lessons from great entrepreneurs.

199.   Write an inspiring message for a professional greeting card.

200.   Imagine a motivational poster with a powerful quote and visual.

CHAPTER 2. COMPUTER SCIENCE AND SOFTWARE DEVELOPMENT

Introduction: AI is Revolutionizing Computing and Software Development

Software development is undergoing a major transformation thanks to artificial intelligence. What used to take **hours of coding, testing, and debugging** can now be accomplished in minutes with the help of advanced AI tools. Far from being a mere trend, AI is becoming an **indispensable companion for developers** , allowing them to optimize their work, speed up processes, and strengthen system security.

Tools like **GitHub Copilot and Codeium** now allow for **automatic code generation** , reducing the cognitive load on programmers and increasing their productivity. AI **also assists in error detection and correction** , identifying bugs before they cause critical issues.

In **Cybersecurity** , machine learning algorithms can anticipate and **detect intrusions** with unparalleled speed and accuracy, thereby strengthening the protection of data and digital infrastructures. **Software testing automation** , once a long and repetitive process, now makes it possible to identify

vulnerabilities and optimize code quality in real time.
Finally, the **optimization of algorithms and systems** through AI opens the way to more efficient, faster software that is better adapted to user needs.

In this chapter, we'll explore **how AI is transforming IT and software development** , and offer you **concrete tips** on how to leverage these technologies to your advantage. Whether you're **a developer, cybersecurity engineer, software architect, or simply passionate about tech , you'll discover new perspectives** here to improve your efficiency and innovate in your field .

Get ready to code faster, smarter, and more efficiently with artificial intelligence!

Here are 200 prompts in the field of IT and software development , classified by categories.

1. Programming and Web Development (30 prompts)

1. Explains the difference between a framework and a library in programming.
2. Describe how REST APIs work and give an example implementation.
3. Write a tutorial on how to build a website with React and Node.js.

4. Compare the advantages and disadvantages of Python and JavaScript for web development.

5. Offers a development project in PHP and Laravel.

6. Explains how to optimize website performance with Lighthouse.

7. Describe how the DOM works and how it interacts with JavaScript.

8. Shows how to use Tailwind CSS to style a web application.

9. Explains the differences between SQL and NoSQL databases.

10. Write a guide on how to build a GraphQL API with Apollo Server.

11. Provides a hands-on exercise on authenticating with Firebase.

12. Shows how to create a static website with Jekyll or Hugo.

13. Write an article about modern web architectures (monolithic vs microservices).

14. Explains how to manage global state with Redux or Vuex.

15. Write a tutorial on Progressive Web Apps (PWA).

16. Describes best security practices in web development.

17. Shows how to use Docker to deploy a web

application.

18. Explains the usefulness of WebSockets and gives an example in Node.js.

19. Provides a guide to code versioning with Git and GitHub.

20. Write a tutorial on how to build a full-stack application with MERN.

21. Compare the advantages of Django and Flask in Python.

22. Describe the importance of accessibility (a11y) in web development.

23. Explains how to use OAuth2 to secure an API.

24. Write a detailed guide on optimizing SQL queries.

25. Shows how to deploy a Next.js project to Vercel.

26. Explains memory management in JavaScript and the garbage collector.

27. Write a tutorial on CI/CD deployment with GitHub Actions.

28. Describe the different caching strategies in a web application.

29. Explains the MVC architecture and gives an example implementation.

30. Write a comparison of the most popular databases in 2025.

2. Artificial Intelligence and Machine Learning (30 prompts)

31. Describe how artificial neural networks work.
32. Explains how to train a machine learning model with Scikit-Learn.
33. Shows how to use TensorFlow for image classification.
34. Compare the differences between supervised and unsupervised learning.
35. Offers a hands-on project in computer vision.
36. Write a guide on NLP (Natural Language Processing) and its applications.
37. Shows how to use OpenAI GPT to generate text.
38. Explains how a clustering model like K-Means works.
39. Provides an implementation of anomaly detection with Python.
40. Describe the importance of data quality in AI.
41. Explains GANs (Generative Adversarial Networks) and their applications.
42. Write a tutorial on training a chatbot with Rasa.
43. Shows how to use Hugging Face to fine-tune

an NLP model.

44. Proposes an AI project in the field of Cybersecurity.

45. Compares the most used AI frameworks (PyTorch, TensorFlow, Keras).

46. Describe the ethical challenges associated with artificial intelligence.

47. Explains the concept of reinforcement learning with an example in Python.

48. Writes a guide on hyperparameter optimization in ML.

49. Shows how to implement a facial recognition model.

50. Proposes an approach to explain a deep learning model (Explainable AI).

51. Describe the advantages and disadvantages of generative AI.

52. Shows how to use AutoML to create a model without coding.

53. Explains how to do time series prediction with LSTM.

54. Write an article about AI in the medical field.

55. Describe modern deep learning model architectures (Transformers, CNN, RNN).

56. Explains how to use Google Colab to train an AI model.

57. Shows how to test an AI model to avoid

overfitting.

58. Proposes an AI project in sentiment analysis on Twitter.

59. Describe the steps of data preprocessing in machine learning.

60. Write an article on AI trends for the next 5 years.

3. Cybersecurity and Ethical Hacking (20 prompts)

61. Explains the basics of encryption and SSL certificates.

62. Shows how to secure a web application against XSS and CSRF attacks.

63. Write a guide on Penetration Testing.

64. Compares the main encryption protocols.

65. Describe brute force techniques and how to prevent them.

66. Shows how to configure a firewall with UFW on Linux.

67. Explains internet anonymity and the use of VPNs.

68. Write a guide to the main phishing attacks.

69. Describe how the dark web and cybercriminals work.

70. Shows how to use Kali Linux to test the security of a network.

71. Write an article about ransomware and how to protect yourself from it.
72. Compares major cybersecurity tools (Metasploit , Wireshark , Burp Suite).
73. Explains the importance of multi-factor authentication (MFA).
74. Provides a guide to managing secure passwords.
75. Describe how honeypots work in cybersecurity.
76. Write an article about the latest global cyber attacks.
77. Explains the basics of protecting APIs from DDoS attacks .
78. Shows how to encrypt a hard drive in Linux.
79. forensic techniques in cybercrime analysis.
80. Explains the impact of AI in modern cybersecurity.

4. DevOps and Cloud Computing (20 prompts)

81. DevOps cycle and its benefits.
82. Shows how to set up a CI/CD pipeline with Jenkins.
83. Explains virtualization and containers (Docker vs. VM).
84. Compare AWS, Google Cloud and Azure.

85. Demonstrates how to deploy a serverless application with AWS Lambda.

86. Write a guide on Kubernetes and container orchestration.

87. Describe best practices for monitoring in DevOps .

88. Compare Terraform and Ansible for infrastructure management.

89. Explains how a microservices architecture works.

90. Describes how to optimize the cost of a cloud infrastructure.

5. Mobile Development (20 prompts)

91. Explains the differences between native, hybrid, and PWA development.

92. Shows how to build a mobile app with Flutter.

93. Compare React Native and Swift for iOS app development.

94. Explains how to optimize the performance of a mobile application.

95. Write a tutorial on implementing Firebase in a mobile app.

96. Describe how push notifications work with OneSignal .

97. app payment with Stripe .

98. Explains how to use SQLite for local storage in mobile.

99. Write a guide on how to publish an app on the App Store and Google Play.

100.   Describe the UX/UI design principles for mobile applications.

101.   Shows how to manage authentication with Google and Facebook on mobile.

102.   Explains how to create an offline mode in a mobile application.

103.   Compare Kotlin and Java for Android development.

104.   Shows how to use GraphQL with a mobile application.

105.   Write an article about mobile development trends in 2025.

106.   Explains how to test a mobile application with Appium .

107.   Describe the importance of accessibility in mobile applications.

108.   Propose a mobile application project in SwiftUI .

109.   Shows how to integrate an interactive map with Google Maps API.

110.   Explains how to monetize a mobile app with advertising.

6. Databases and Big Data (20 prompts)

111.   Compares relational and non-relational databases.

112.   Explains how indexing works in SQL databases.

113.   Shows how to create an optimized database with PostgreSQL.

114.   Describe the principles of normalization in databases.

115.   Explains how to use MongoDB for a NoSQL application.

116.   Shows how to perform database replication with MySQL.

117.   Write a guide on database modeling.

118.   Compare Hadoop and Spark for big data processing.

119.   Shows how to use Apache Kafka for data streaming.

120.   Explains the concept of distributed databases.

121.   Describes how to secure a database against SQL injection.

122.   Propose a data analysis project with Pandas and SQL.

123.   Shows how to manage database

transactions.

124.   Explains how to do data warehousing with Snowflake .

125.   Compares JSON, XML, and Parquet data storage formats.

126.   Write a guide on optimizing SQL queries.

127.   Shows how to use Redis as a cache to improve performance.

128.   Explains how graph databases (Neo4j) work.

129.   Write an article about how databases will evolve in 2025.

7. Blockchain and Cryptocurrencies (15 prompts)

130.   Explains how blockchain works and its applications.

131.   Shows how to create a smart contract with Solidity and Ethereum .

132.   Compare Bitcoin, Ethereum and alternative cryptocurrencies .

133.   Describe the concept of proof of work and proof of stake.

134.   Explains how an NFT works and how to create one.

135.   Shows how to store and secure

cryptocurrencies .

136.   Write a guide on how to implement a crypto wallet .

137.   Describe the challenges associated with blockchain scalability .

138.   Explains how DAOs (Decentralized Autonomous Organizations).

139.   Demonstrates how to use Hyperledger for private blockchain solutions.

140.   cryptocurrency regulation in 2025.

141.   Explains how to develop a Web3 application.

142.   Describe the risks and issues associated with smart contracts .

143.   Shows how to interact with the blockchain using Web3.js.

144.   Compare different blockchain platforms (Ethereum , Solana, Cardano).

8. Systems and Networks (20 prompts)

145.   Explains how TCP/IP networks work.

146.   Describe the differences between IPv4 and IPv6.

147.   Shows how to setup a Linux server with Apache and Nginx .

148.   Write a guide on VPNs and how they work.

149.   Compares HTTP and HTTPS protocols.

150.   Describe how firewalls and proxies work.

151.   Explains how DNS works and its role on the Internet.

152.   Shows how to set up a secure network for a business.

153.   load balancer works and its advantages.

154.   Explains how to set up a secure FTP server.

155.   Shows how to use SSH to secure access to a remote server.

156.   Describe the most common network attacks and how to avoid them.

157.   Write a guide on virtualization with VMware and VirtualBox .

158.   Explains how BGP works and its role on the Internet.

159.   Shows how to analyze network traffic with Wireshark .

160.   Compare network storage technologies (NAS vs SAN).

161.   Describe how network redundancy works to ensure high availability.

162.   Explains the concept of SDN (Software -Defined Networking).

163.   Shows how to set up a network architecture for a data center .

164.   Write a guide on the basics of cloud networking.

9. Automation and Scripting (15 prompts)

165.   Explains how to automate tasks with Python.

166.   Bash script to manage files on Linux.

167.   Describe the differences between PowerShell and Bash .

168.   Explains how to use Ansible to automate infrastructure deployment.

169.   Shows how to create a Telegram bot with Python.

170.   Write a tutorial on Selenium for web test automation.

171.   most popular scripting languages in 2025.

172.   Explains how to use cron to

automate tasks on a Linux server.

173.   Shows how to write an automation script for AWS with Boto3.

174.   Describe best practices for writing a secure shell script.

175.   Explains how to automate application deployment with Terraform .

176.   Shows how to use Puppeteer for web scraping .

177.   Compare IT automation tools (Puppet , Chef, Ansible).

178.   Write a guide on creating scripts for log management.

179.   Explains how to integrate a Discord bot in Python.

10. Quantum Computing and the Future of Tech (10 prompts)

180.   Explains the principles of quantum computing.

181.   Compare the most popular quantum algorithms.

182.   Shows how to use Qiskit to program a quantum computer.

183.   Describe the potential impact of quantum computing on cybersecurity.

184.   Explains how qubits differ from

traditional bits.

185.　　　　Write an article on current challenges in quantum computing.

186.　　　Describe leading companies in quantum research.

187.　　　　Shows how a quantum algorithm can accelerate machine learning.

188.　　　Compare quantum computers and classical supercomputers.

189.　　　Write a guide to key concepts of quantum physics as applied to IT.

11. Miscellaneous and Technological Trends (11 prompts)

190.　　　　Analyzes emerging trends in cybersecurity for the coming years.

191.　　　　Explains the impact of Edge Computing on the Internet of Things (IoT).

192.　　　Compare artificial intelligence and generative artificial intelligence.

193.　　　　Describe how 5G is transforming application development and cloud services.

194.　　　Shows how to use Low-Code and No-Code to accelerate application development.

195. Explains how businesses are using AI to optimize IT infrastructures.

196. Describe the concept of "Digital Twin" and its applications in computing.

197. Write a guide to the best IT certifications for 2025.

198. Explains the role of IT in the energy transition and digital ecology.

199. Shows how serverless architecture works and its benefits.

200. Write an article about the future of brain-machine interfaces (BCIs) and their impact on computing.

CHAPTER 3. MEDICINE AND HEALTH

Introduction: Artificial Intelligence in the Service of Medicine and Health

Artificial intelligence (AI) is revolutionizing the field of medicine and healthcare. Thanks to technological advances, it now makes it possible to **improve the accuracy of diagnoses, accelerate medical research, optimize patient care and enhance the efficiency of surgical interventions** . This upheaval offers invaluable opportunities for healthcare professionals, allowing them to offer **faster, more precise and better adapted care to the needs of patients** .

AI does not replace doctors, but it acts as **a powerful assistant** , providing them with decision-making tools, automating complex tasks and facilitating the interpretation of large medical data.

In this collection of **prompts dedicated to AI in medicine and health** , we will explore several areas where artificial intelligence plays a key role:

- **AI-assisted diagnosis** : Using machine learning, AI can analyze medical exams like X-rays, ultrasounds, or MRIs to help doctors identify pathologies with high accuracy.

- **Drug development and biomedical research** : AI accelerates the discovery of new treatments by analyzing huge databases and identifying promising molecules.

- **Medical Image Analysis** : AI enables faster and more reliable reading of medical images, reducing the risk of diagnostic errors.

- **Assisting surgeons through robotics** : AI-assisted surgical robots improve the precision of operations and enable less invasive procedures.

- **Patient monitoring and personalized medicine** : Thanks to connected sensors and AI algorithms, doctors can monitor patients' health status in real time and adapt treatments according to their specific needs.

AI represents a major advancement in the medical field, and its potential continues to grow. **This prompt guide will help you explore all these applications and leverage artificial intelligence to improve medical practice and patient care.**

Here are 200 prompts that can be used in the field of Medicine and Health , divided into different categories.

1. General Medicine and Pathologies

(30 prompts)

1. Explains the causes and treatments of type 2 diabetes.
2. Describe the symptoms and treatments of high blood pressure.
3. Compare the different types of cardiovascular diseases.
4. Explains the risk factors for breast cancer.
5. Describe the early symptoms of Alzheimer's disease.
6. Compare flu and COVID-19 in terms of symptoms and prevention.
7. Write a guide on stroke prevention.
8. Explains the different types of diabetes and their impacts on health.
9. Describe how the immune system works.
10. Shows how to detect the early signs of colorectal cancer.
11. Explains the importance of sleep for cardiovascular health.
12. Compares drug and natural treatments for anxiety.
13. Describe the possible complications of obesity.
14. Explains the links between chronic stress and autoimmune diseases.
15. Describe the causes and treatments of

chronic migraines.

16. Compare conventional medicine and alternative medicine.

17. Explains how to recognize a food allergy.

18. Describe common side effects of antibiotics.

19. Explains how to prevent infectious diseases while traveling.

20. Compare the different types of vaccines and how they work.

21. Writes a guide on managing hypothyroidism.

22. Explains how gene therapy works.

23. Describe the impacts of air pollution on respiratory health.

24. Explains the role of the gut microbiota in overall health.

25. Compare the different forms of arthritis and their treatments.

26. Shows how to manage a chronic illness on a daily basis.

27. Explains the effects of dehydration on the body.

28. Describe the health benefits of intermittent fasting.

29. Explains how to detect a rare disease.

30. Write an article about the evolution of cancer treatments.

2. Nutrition and Food (20 prompts)

31. Explains the health benefits of omega-3.

32. Compare the Mediterranean diet and the ketogenic diet.

33. Describe the importance of dietary fiber in the diet.

34. Explains the dangers of ultra-processed foods.

35. Write a guide to superfoods and their benefits.

36. Compare the health effects of white sugar and honey.

37. Explains how to adopt an anti-inflammatory diet.

38. Describe the best plant-based sources of protein.

39. Compare intermittent fasting and prolonged fasting.

40. Explains how to avoid nutritional deficiencies in vegetarians.

41. Describe the role of magnesium in the body.

42. Explains why hydration is essential for digestion.

43. Compare the benefits of probiotics and prebiotics.

44. Explains the impact of gluten on gut health.

45. Describe the effects of caffeine on

metabolism.

46. Write a guide on reading food labels.
47. Explains why antioxidants are important for health.
48. Describe how diet can influence mental health.
49. Compare natural and artificial sweeteners.
50. Explains the importance of essential amino acids.

3. Mental Health and Psychology (20 prompts)

51. Explains the differences between stress, anxiety and depression.
52. Describe the signs of professional burnout.
53. Compare cognitive therapy and behavioral therapy.
54. Explains the effects of meditation on the brain.
55. Shows how to practice mindfulness in everyday life.
56. Describe the benefits of physical activity on mental health.
57. Explains the mechanisms of screen addiction.
58. Compare bipolar disorder and schizophrenia.

59. Write a guide on how to manage panic attacks.

60. Explains how to improve emotional resilience.

61. Describe the impacts of lack of sleep on mental health.

62. Explains how to develop a mental wellness routine.

63. Compare the effects of acute stress and chronic stress.

64. Describe the different types of phobias and their treatments.

65. Explains how to overcome psychological trauma.

66. Shows how to improve self-esteem with simple exercises.

67. Describe the impacts of social media on mental health.

68. Compare psychiatry and clinical psychology.

69. Explains how diet influences mood and cognition.

70. Describe the importance of managing emotions for good mental health.

4. Sports Medicine and Rehabilitation (20 prompts)

71. Explains the benefits of weight training on bone health.

72. Compare static and dynamic stretching for muscle recovery.

73. Describe how to prevent running injuries.

74. Explains how to optimize your cardiovascular training.

75. Shows how to use cryotherapy for muscle recovery.

76. Compare different types of proteins for post-exercise recovery.

77. Describe the impacts of a sedentary lifestyle on muscle health.

78. Explains how to strengthen your immune system through sport.

79. Write a guide on preventing tendonitis.

80. Compare yoga and Pilates for mobility and rehabilitation.

5. Medical Innovations and Health of the Future (20 prompts)

81. Explains how artificial intelligence is transforming medicine.

82. Describe the benefits and limitations of telemedicine.

83. Compare traditional vaccines and mRNA vaccines.

84. Explains how nanotechnology is used in medicine.

85. Describe the potential of 3D printed organs.

86. Shows how robotics improves surgery.

87. Compare DNA tests and their usefulness in preventive medicine.

88. Explains how virtual reality is used in rehabilitation.

89. Describe the ethical issues surrounding genetic modification.

90. Write a guide on personalized medicine and its benefits.

6. Emergency Medicine and First Aid (20 prompts)

91. Explains how to perform cardiopulmonary resuscitation (CPR).

92. Describe the actions to take in the event of choking.

93. Shows how to react to an epileptic seizure.

94. Explains the steps for treating a serious burn.

95. Compare first aid for a fracture and a sprain.

96. Describe how to stop heavy bleeding.

97. Explains first aid in case of drowning.

98. Describe how to care for an unconscious

person.

99. Shows how to recognize a stroke and react quickly.

100.   Compare the different types of dressings and their uses.

101.   Explains how to manage acute food poisoning.

102.   Describe how to administer an adrenaline injection for severe allergies.

103.   Explains the risks and management of anaphylactic shock.

104.   Compare emergency treatments for severe hypoglycemia.

105.   Explains how to recognize a concussion.

106.   Describe the procedures to follow in the event of a road accident.

107.   Shows how to handle a snake or venomous animal bite.

108.   Explains how to treat a deep cut without immediate medical assistance.

109.   Describe first aid for severe hypothermia.

110.   Explains how to prepare for a medical emergency at home.

7. Public Health and Epidemiology (20 prompts)

111.   Explains the differences between an epidemic, a pandemic and an endemic.

112.   Describe mass vaccination strategies and their impact.

113.   Shows how antibiotic resistance is a global problem.

114.   Explains how governments respond to health crises.

115.   Compares the public health systems of different countries.

116.   Describe the impacts of climate change on human health.

117.   Explains the role of epidemiologists in the management of infectious diseases.

118.   Shows how zoonotic diseases emerge and spread.

119.   Describe the challenges of access to care in developing countries.

120.   Explains the impact of public health policies on longevity.

121.   Compares prevention approaches against cardiovascular diseases.

122.   Describe how pandemics impact global economies.

123.   Explains the role of global

organizations in combating disease.

124.		Compare tobacco and alcohol prevention campaigns.

125.		Describe the influence of social media on perceptions of vaccines.

126.		Explains why some eradicated diseases come back.

127.		Shows how early detection tests save lives.

128.		Describe the role of medical databases in epidemiological research.

129.		Explains the controversies surrounding alternative medicine and public health.

130.		Compares methods of tracing infectious diseases throughout history.

8. Health and Aging (20 prompts)

131.		Explains how to slow down cellular aging naturally.

132.		Describe the benefits of omega-3 for the aging brain.

133.		Shows how to maintain good bone density after age 50.

134.		Compare the different methods of treating osteoarthritis.

135.		Explains the factors that influence longevity.

136.   Describe how to prevent age-related memory loss.

137.   Shows the impact of sport on brain aging.

138.   Compare hormone therapies for menopause.

139.   Explains the importance of vitamin D in seniors.

140.   Describe the early signs of senile dementia.

141.   Shows how a healthy lifestyle extends life expectancy.

142.   Compare the benefits of the Mediterranean diet for seniors.

143.   Explains how to avoid sarcopenia as you age.

144.   Describe the best strategies for restful sleep after age 60.

145.   Explains the impact of stress on premature aging.

146.   Shows how music helps prevent cognitive decline.

147.   Describe technologies that improve the quality of life of older adults.

148.   Explains how to adapt diet to the needs of seniors.

149.   Shows how to avoid social isolation in older people.

150. Compare new advances in anti-aging medicine.

9. Neuroscience and Brain Functioning (20 prompts)

151. Explains how the brain learns new skills.

152. Describe the effects of lack of sleep on memory.

153. Compare the brain of an adult and that of a developing child.

154. Explains how the hippocampus plays a key role in memory.

155. Describe the impacts of drugs on the brain.

156. Shows how emotions influence decision making.

157. Compares brain plasticity in young people and adults.

158. Explains how the brain responds to chronic stress.

159. Describe the role of neurotransmitters in regulating mood.

160. Explains how artificial intelligence is used in neuroscience.

161. Describe how physical exercise improves brain health.

162.   Explains how meditation changes brain activity.

163.   Shows how video games influence brain development.

164.   Compare how the brain of an introvert and an extrovert works.

165.   Explains how the brain processes pain.

166.   Describe the effects of screens on concentration and cognition.

167.   Shows how music stimulates certain areas of the brain.

168.   Explains how neurodegenerative disorders affect neurons.

169.   Describe the links between sleep and memory consolidation.

170.   Compares existing therapies to treat neurological disorders.

10. Medical Technologies and Innovations (20 prompts)

171.   Explains how telemedicine is revolutionizing healthcare.

172.   Describe the benefits of brain implants in treating neurological diseases.

173.   Shows how surgical robots

improve the precision of operations.

174.   Compares the different types of cell therapies in regenerative medicine.

175.   Explains how 3D printing is used to make artificial organs.

176.   Describe the role of nanorobots in medical treatments.

177.   Shows how artificial intelligence helps in early diagnosis of diseases.

178.   Compare new approaches to personalized medicine.

179.   Explains how exoskeletons assist paralyzed people.

180.   Describe how biosensors can improve medical monitoring.

181.   Shows how clinical trials have evolved thanks to digital technologies.

182.   Explains how medical databases facilitate clinical research.

183.   Compare the different types of bionic prosthetics.

184.   Describe the impact of connected objects on preventive health.

185.   Explains how gene therapies can treat certain genetic diseases.

186.   Describe advances in cancer therapies.

187.   microbiota analysis helps to

understand certain pathologies.

188.   Explains how blockchain secures medical records.

189.   Describe the ethical challenges associated with augmented medicine.

190.   Compare retinal implants to restore vision.

11. Alternative Medicine and Wellness (10 prompts)

191.   Explains the benefits and limitations of acupuncture.

192.   Compares the effectiveness of herbal remedies with conventional drugs.

193.   Describe the role of aromatherapy in stress management.

194.   Explains how yoga can improve cardiovascular health.

195.   Shows how therapeutic massages influence overall well-being.

196.   Compares different traditional medicine practices around the world.

197.   Describe the impact of meditation on chronic pain management.

198.   Explains how homeopathy is perceived in the scientific world.

199.   Shows how naturopathy can

complement conventional medicine.

200.   Describe precautions to take
before trying an alternative therapy.

CHAPTER 4.FINANCE AND ECONOMICS

Introduction: Artificial Intelligence at the Heart of Finance and the Economy

Artificial intelligence (AI) has become an **essential tool in the world of finance and economics** , where speed and accuracy of analysis are essential. Thanks to advanced algorithms and machine learning, AI can now process huge volumes of data in real time, identify trends invisible to the human eye, and automate complex financial decisions.

Whether it's **financial market analysis, risk management, fraud detection or investment optimization** , AI plays a key role in modernizing and making economic systems more efficient. It enables businesses, investors and financial institutions to **make more informed decisions, improve their profitability and minimize risks** .

In this collection of prompts dedicated to finance and economics , we will explore several areas of application of AI:

- **Financial Market Analysis and Prediction** :

AI is able to analyze market fluctuations in real time, identify trends and anticipate stock market movements using advanced predictive models.

- **Banking Fraud Detection** : Using machine learning, AI can spot suspicious transactions and prevent fraud by analyzing unusual activity patterns.

- **Automation of investment advice (robo-advisors)** : Intelligent algorithms help investors manage their portfolio by offering them strategies adapted to their profile and their financial objectives.

- **Credit Scoring and Risk Management** : AI helps assess borrowers' creditworthiness with increased accuracy, reducing the risk of default for financial institutions.

- **Optimizing financial management** : Artificial intelligence helps businesses and individuals better manage their budgets, reduce costs and maximize profits by analyzing their financial flows.

Artificial intelligence is profoundly transforming finance and economics, making decisions faster , **more accurate and more personalized** . This prompts guide will provide you with the tools you need to exploit the full potential of AI in these areas and **optimize your financial strategies with the most advanced technologies** .

Here are 200 prompts that can be used in the field of Finance and Economics , divided into several subcategories.

1. Personal Finance (25 prompts)

1. Explains the importance of budget management for good financial health.
2. Describe the best strategies for saving effectively each month.
3. Compare the advantages and disadvantages of a savings account and a checking account.
4. Explains how to create a balanced budget using the 50/30/20 rule.
5. Provides advice on how to avoid over-indebtedness and better manage your credit.
6. Describe the financial habits of financially independent people.
7. Shows how to automate your finances to avoid management errors.
8. Analyze best practices to pay off your debts faster.
9. Explains how to improve your credit score and why it's important.
10. Describe common mistakes to avoid when managing your personal finances.

11. Compare the advantages and disadvantages of credit cards and debit cards.

12. Explains how to set up an emergency fund and how much savings to put into it.

13. Describe the best ways to optimize your spending to save money.

14. Compare different investment methods suitable for beginners.

15. Explains how to manage finances as a couple and avoid money conflicts.

16. Describe the importance of financial education from an early age.

17. Explains how to use psychology to improve your finances.

18. Compare different retirement savings strategies and their tax advantages.

19. Provides advice on dealing with a personal financial crisis.

20. Explains how to avoid the most common financial scams and frauds.

21. Describe the best mobile apps for managing your personal finances.

22. Explains how to negotiate your salary and maximize your income.

23. Shows how financial minimalism can improve economic stability.

24. Describe how to create a passive income stream to achieve financial freedom.

25. Analyzes the impacts of inflation on personal savings and how to protect yourself from it.

2. Investment and Stock Market (25 prompts)

26. Explains the basic principles of the stock market.
27. Describe the differences between stocks, bonds, and ETFs.
28. Explains the importance of diversifying an investment portfolio.
29. Analyzes long term vs short term investment strategies.
30. Compare passive investing and active investing.
31. Describe the best platforms for investing in the stock market as a beginner.
32. Explains how to analyze a company before investing in its shares.
33. Compares trading strategies : scalping, day trading, swing trading.
34. Describe the criteria to consider before investing in real estate.
35. Explains the benefits and risks of cryptocurrencies as an investment.
36. Describe the impact of interest rates on

financial investments.

37. Explains how leverage works in trading.

38. Analyzes the most important stock indices and their meaning.

39. Describe business cycles and their impact on investments.

40. Explains the best strategies to minimize risk in the stock market.

41. Compare investing in rental properties and investing in stocks.

42. Explains how dividends work and how to profit from them.

43. Describe current trends in sustainable investing (ESG).

44. Compare the advantages and disadvantages of IPOs and SPACs .

45. Explains how to protect your investment portfolio in times of crisis.

46. Describe the role of hedges funds and their influence on financial markets.

47. Explains how to use financial ratios to value a business.

48. Compare investing in precious metals and investing in cryptocurrencies .

49. Explains how to invest in artificial intelligence and new technologies.

50. Describe common mistakes beginner investors make and how to avoid them.

3.   Global   Economy   and Macroeconomics (25 prompts)

51. Explains the role of central banks in the global economy.
52. Describe the effects of globalization on national economies.
53. Analyzes the causes and consequences of inflation.
54. Compare capitalism, socialism and communism in economic terms.
55. Explains how public debt affects economic growth.
56. Describe the impact of financial crises on the global economy.
57. Explains the differences between GDP, GNP and GNI.
58. Analyzes economic cycles and how they influence markets.
59. Describe the role of the IMF and the World Bank in the global economy.
60. Compares monetary and fiscal policies and their impact.
61. Explains how unemployment is calculated and what it means for an economy.
62. Describe the effect of economic sanctions on a country.

63. Compare the effects of currency devaluation and revaluation.

64. Explains the impact of exchange rates on international trade.

65. Analyzes the role of multinationals in the global economy.

66. Explains why some emerging economies are growing rapidly.

67. Describe the factors that influence the value of a currency.

68. Compare the economic models of the United States, Europe and China.

69. Explains how new technologies are transforming the global economy.

70. Describe the economic issues linked to the energy transition.

71. Analyzes the impact of fiscal policies on economic growth.

72. Explains how corruption affects economic development.

73. Compare the different economic crises of the last 100 years.

74. Analyzes the impact of financial innovations on the global economy.

75. Describe how startups are disrupting traditional markets.

4. Cryptocurrencies and FinTech (25

prompts)

76. Explains how Bitcoin works and its impact on finance.

77. Compare the most popular cryptocurrencies and their usefulness.

78. Describe the benefits and risks of blockchain in finance.

79. Explains how cryptocurrency mining works.

80. Analyzes the impact of regulation on the cryptocurrency market .

81. Describe how banks are adopting blockchain technology.

82. Explains the concept of stablecoins and their usefulness.

83. cryptocurrency trading platforms .

84. Describe the best strategies for investing in cryptocurrencies .

85. cryptocurrency assets .

86. Compare ICOs, IDOs and STOs in the crypto universe .

87. Analyzes the impact of smart contracts on the digital economy.

88. Describe the current limitations of blockchain and possible solutions.

89. Explains how NFTs are transforming the digital economy.

90. Compare decentralized finance (DeFi) and traditional finance.

91. Describe how banks are adapting to the rise of cryptocurrencies .

92. Explains why some cryptos are more volatile than others.

93. Describe the trends to watch in crypto.

94. Explains how asset tokenization is changing investing.

95. Compare hot and cold crypto wallets.

96. Analyzes the role of metaverses in the digital economy.

97. Explains how to spot scams in the crypto world.

98. Compare different blockchains in terms of speed and cost.

99. Describe the future of digital finance.

100.   Explains how cryptocurrencies influence financial geopolitics.

5.   Financial   Education   and Investment Strategies (25 prompts)

101.   Describe the importance of financial education from childhood.

102.   Explains how to develop a long-term investing mindset.

103.   Describes the best resources for

learning how to invest in the stock market.

104.   Analyzes the importance of understanding risks before making financial investments.

105.   Explains how to determine your investor profile.

106.   Compares investment strategies for young adults and those nearing retirement.

107.   Explains why diversification is essential for an investment portfolio.

108.   Shows how investing in index funds can be a profitable long-term strategy.

109.   Explains the impact of management fees on investment returns.

110.   Describe the differences between passive and active investing.

111.   Analyzes the impact of interest rates on real estate investments.

112.   Compares investments in stocks and bonds in terms of return and risk.

113.   Explains the benefits of real estate investments in a diversified portfolio.

114.   Provides advice for investing in times of economic volatility.

115.   Explains how to use stock

indices to analyze the market.

116.   Shows how to calculate the return on a stock investment.

117.   Describe the advantages and disadvantages of investing in commodities.

118.   Explains the fundamental principles of ethical and responsible investing.

119.   Compare different types of investment accounts for individuals.

120.   Explains how investing in cryptocurrencies differs from traditional investments.

121.   Describe common mistakes beginner investors make and how to avoid them.

122.   Shows how financial planning can help achieve long-term goals.

123.   Explains the benefits of automating investments through robo-advisors.

124.   Describe the investment strategies used by institutional investors.

125.   Explains how market timing affects long-term investment performance.

6. Financial Markets and Behavioral

Economics (25 prompts)

126. Describe the major current trends in global financial markets.

127. Explains the impact of emotions on financial decision making.

128. Analyzes the cognitive biases that influence individuals' investment choices.

129. Describe how economic crises affect investor psychology.

130. Explains how financial markets react to major economic announcements.

131. Compares behavioral finance theories with traditional finance.

132. Describe the effects of asset overvaluation on the overall economy.

133. Analyzes the role of financial media in market perception.

134. Describe the principles of efficient market theory.

135. Explains the importance of risk management in financial decision making.

136. Analyzes the role of institutional investors in financial markets.

137. Compares different approaches to economic forecasting in behavioral

finance.

138.   Describe economic events that trigger changes in market sentiment.

139.   Explains how leverage can amplify risks in financial markets.

140.   Shows how governments influence financial markets with tax policies.

141.   Describe the factors that influence stock price fluctuations.

142.   Explains the impact of interest rates on investor psychology.

143.   Compare socially responsible investing with traditional investing.

144.   Analyzes trends in ESG investments and their influence on financial markets.

145.   Describe the strategies of investors who successfully outperform the market.

146.   Explains the effects of business cycles on consumer behavior.

147.   Compares stock and bond returns over several decades.

148.   Analyzes the impact of monetary policies on the stability of financial markets.

149.   Describe how inflation

influences investment decisions.

150.   Explains how exchange rates can affect the profitability of multinational companies.

7. International Finance and World Trade (25 prompts)

151.   Explains the impact of trade policy on the global economy.

152.   Describe the role of international trade agreements in regulating financial markets.

153.   Analyzes the impact of the trade war between two major economies on the global market.

154.   Compares major financial systems in developed and emerging economies.

155.   Describe the economic consequences of the United Kingdom leaving the European Union.

156.   Analyzes the effects of the currency war on the global economy.

157.   Explains how foreign investment affects a country's economic growth.

158.   Compares international financial regulations to combat money

laundering.

159.   Describe the effects of economic sanctions on global trade.

160.   Analyzes the impact of exchange rates on exports and imports.

161.   Explains how global economic crises affect emerging markets.

162.   Describe the advantages and disadvantages of free trade zones.

163.   Explains the role of international banks in facilitating global trade.

164.   Compares market economies and planned economies in an international context.

165.   Analyzes the economic issues of trade between the United States and China.

166.   Describe the effects of globalization on the competitiveness of national companies.

167.   Explains the impact of foreign direct investment on the local economy.

168.   Describe the economic challenges facing developing countries in the face of external debt.

169.   Analyzes the impact of international tax policies on multinational enterprises.

170.   Explains how the monetary policy of major economic powers influences the global economy.

171.   Compares different types of financial markets in developing economies.

172.   Describe the impact of technological innovations on international trade.

173.   Explains how international treaties influence tax regulations.

174.   Analyzes the effects of global interest rates on international investments.

175.   Describe the consequences of deglobalization on the world economy.

8.   Development Economics and Sustainable Progress (25 prompts)

176.   Describe the factors that contribute to the economic development of developing countries.

177.   Compare the economic policies put in place to reduce poverty.

178.   Analyzes the impact of climate change on the global economy.

179.   Explains how innovation can promote economic growth in emerging

countries.

180.   Describe economic policies aimed at reducing income inequality.

181.   Compare the different approaches to sustainable development in economics.

182.   Explains how investing in education can boost economic development.

183.   Analyzes the economic issues linked to the energy transition towards renewable energies.

184.   Describe the impact of infrastructure investments on economic growth.

185.   Compares economic development strategies in Africa, Asia and Latin America.

186.   Explains the effects of government subsidies on local industries.

187.   Describe the roles of microfinance in emerging economies.

188.   Analyzes the effects of trade policies on developing countries.

189.   Explains the role of international organizations in the economic development of poor countries.

190.   Describe the consequences of rapid urbanization on the global economy.

191.   Analyzes the economic benefits of environmental protection policies.

192.   Compares the economic models of capitalism and socialism in a development context.

193.   Explains how tax reforms can promote economic development.

194.   Describe the obstacles to economic growth in developing countries.

195.   Analyzes the impact of digital infrastructure on the competitiveness of developing countries.

196.   Describe the economic issues related to the sustainability of global food systems.

197.   Explains the importance of international cooperation for sustainable development.

198.   Analyzes the effects of financing development through foreign investment.

199.   Describe economic initiatives to improve access to safe drinking water in developing countries.

200.   Compares economic strategies to combat climate change in advanced and developing economies.

CHAPTER 5.EDUCATION AND TRAINING

Introduction: Artificial Intelligence in the Service of Education and Training

Artificial intelligence (AI) is profoundly transforming **education and training** , offering new learning methods that are more interactive, personalized and accessible. Thanks to technological advances, teachers, trainers and learners can now benefit from **intelligent tools** that facilitate the transmission and acquisition of knowledge.

AI can **analyze student performance** , offer content adapted to their level, automate the creation of educational materials, and even break down language barriers through machine translation. Its integration into education not only improves teaching effectiveness, but also learner engagement.

In this collection of **prompts dedicated to education and training** , we will explore several key applications of AI:

- **Virtual tutors and learning assistants** : Chatbots and AI assistants can answer students' questions, guide them through their revisions, and provide personalized support.

- **Creation of interactive and personalized online courses** : AI makes it possible to generate educational content adapted to the needs of learners, by integrating videos, interactive quizzes and exercises adapted to their level.

- **Student performance analysis** : Thanks to machine learning algorithms, it is possible to identify learners' strengths and weaknesses and adapt teaching strategies accordingly.

- **Automatic generation of quizzes and teaching materials** : AI can automatically create tests, exercises and course materials based on specific educational programs.

- **Machine translation and transcription** : By facilitating access to content in multiple languages, AI helps democratize learning and make education more inclusive.

Education is an area where **AI can really make a difference** , offering **innovative solutions to improve learning and make knowledge accessible to all** . This prompts guide will provide you with the tools you need to fully exploit the potential of artificial intelligence in teaching and training.

Here are 200 prompts in the field of Education and Training , organized into several categories.

---

1. Pedagogy and Teaching Methods (25 prompts)

1. Describe the benefits of active learning in the classroom.
2. Compare traditional teaching and competency-based teaching.
3. Explains how to adapt teaching to different learning styles.
4. Describe the importance of play in children's learning.
5. Analyze the benefits of the inverted classroom for students.
6. Explains how to use differentiated instruction to meet student needs.
7. Describe the advantages and disadvantages of formative assessment methods.
8. Explains how to promote critical thinking in students.
9. Analyzes the importance of constructive feedback in education.
10. Describe strategies for motivating struggling students.
11. Explains the role of neuroscience in improving teaching methods.

12. Compare Montessori education and traditional education.

13. Analyze the benefits of collaborative work in the classroom.

14. Describe how to integrate project-based learning into an educational program.

15. Explains the benefits of personalized education on academic success.

16. Analyzes how teachers can promote student autonomy.

17. Describe how to improve student engagement using gamification.

18. Compare individual learning and group learning.

19. Explains how to teach problem solving through case studies.

20. Describe techniques to strengthen students' memorization.

21. Analyzes the challenges of teaching science subjects.

22. Explains the importance of storytelling in teaching.

23. Describe how to integrate creativity into learning.

24. Analyzes the effects of interdisciplinary learning on students' understanding.

25. Explains how to manage a heterogeneous class with varying levels.

2. Technology and Digital Education (25 prompts)

26. Describe the impact of technology on student learning.
27. Compare online learning and face-to-face learning.
28. Explains how to use artificial intelligence to improve education.
29. Analyzes the benefits of using tablets and computers in the classroom.
30. Describe how to integrate serious games in education.
31. Explains how augmented reality can revolutionize education.
32. Compare online learning and MOOCs (Massive Open Online Courses).
33. Analyzes the importance of interactive learning platforms.
34. Describe how teachers can use social media for learning.
35. Explains how to create engaging educational content online.
36. Compare learning tools like Kahoot , Quizlet , and Socrative .
37. Describe how gamification improves student engagement.

38. Analyzes the impact of the metaverse on the education of the future.

39. Explains how big data can help personalize learning.

40. Describe how adaptive learning can revolutionize education.

41. Compare learning platforms like Udemy , Coursera, and Khan Academy .

42. Explains the limitations of online learning for young children.

43. Describe how to use podcasts as an educational tool.

44. Analyzes the challenges of cybersecurity in digital learning.

45. Explains how to design an effective online training module.

46. Describe best practices for evaluating the effectiveness of online courses.

47. Analyzes the challenges of distance learning in developing countries.

48. Explains how to integrate digital skills into school curricula.

49. Describe how artificial intelligence can assist teachers.

50. Analyzes the impact of e-learning on the continuing training of professionals.

3. Education and Personal

Development (25 prompts)

51. Explains how to develop emotional intelligence in students.
52. Describe the importance of self-confidence in learning.
53. Analyzes how stress management affects academic success.
54. Describe the best techniques to improve students' concentration.
55. Explains how to teach resilience to children.
56. Compare academic education and emotional education.
57. Analyzes the impact of reading on students' personal development.
58. Describe how to cultivate curiosity and creativity in children.
59. Explains how sport contributes to student well-being.
60. Analyzes the effect of meditation and mindfulness on academic performance.
61. Describe how to foster a growth mindset in students.
62. Explains the importance of moral and civic education.
63. Analyzes the effects of procrastination on academic performance.
64. Describe how to learn to manage your time

effectively.

65. Explains the impact of extracurricular activities on personal development.

66. Compare self-taught learning and supervised learning.

67. Analyzes how educational travel influences open-mindedness.

68. Describe how to teach decision making to young people.

69. Explains the importance of balancing academic and leisure life.

70. Analyzes how intrinsic motivation influences achievement.

71. Describe how to teach financial management to students.

72. Explains how language learning promotes personal development.

73. Analyzes the importance of ethics and values in education.

74. Describe how to encourage entrepreneurship among students.

75. Explains how volunteer experiences strengthen young people's skills.

4. Educational Systems and Reforms (25 prompts)

76. Compare the education systems of different

countries.

77. Analyzes the impacts of educational reforms on academic performance.

78. Describe how to reduce educational inequalities.

79. Explains how to improve teacher training.

80. Compares public and private education in terms of effectiveness.

81. Analyzes the challenges of dropping out of school and how to prevent it.

82. Describe the benefits of multi-level classes.

83. Explains how education can reduce poverty.

84. Compare formal education and informal education.

85. Analyzes the importance of girls' education in developing countries.

86. Describe how to make education more accessible to people with disabilities.

87. Explains the impact of free education on the quality of education.

88. Analyzes the effects of globalization on educational systems.

89. Describe how to improve student academic guidance.

90. Explains the importance of 21st century skills in education.

91. Analyzes how digitalization can transform national education.

92. Compares educational approaches in Asia, Europe and North America.

93. Explains how to strengthen cooperation between parents and teachers.

94. Describe the challenges of education in rural areas.

95. Analyzes the impact of educational policies on student performance.

96. Explains why education must be adapted to the needs of the labor market.

97. Describe how to promote equal opportunities at school.

98. Compare the benefits of the baccalaureate, the international baccalaureate and the American diploma.

99. Explains why education should include lessons on managing emotions.

100. Analyzes the effect of the number of students per class on learning.

5. Professional Training and Continuing Learning (25 prompts)

101. Describe the importance of continuing education for professionals.

102. Analyzes the differences between corporate training and academic training.

103.		Explains how MOOCs are revolutionizing professional training.

104.		Describe best practices for learning new skills quickly.

105.		Compare self-taught training and supervised training.

106.		Explains how to develop an effective adult training program.

107.		Analyzes the challenges of professional retraining and how to overcome them.

108.		Describe how to use mentoring to improve professional skills.

109.		Explains how online training can improve business productivity.

110.		Analyzes the advantages of professional certifications over traditional degrees.

111.		Describe how soft skills influence professional success.

112.		Explains how to integrate microlearning into corporate training.

113.		Compare short and long training courses in companies.

114.		Analyzes the impact of training on employee satisfaction and motivation.

115.		Describe how to measure the effectiveness of professional training.

116.   Explains how businesses can encourage continuous learning.

117.   Analyzes how artificial intelligence can improve vocational training.

118.   Describe best practices for teaching technical skills.

119.   Explains why corporate training must include personal development.

120.   Compare face-to-face training and distance learning in companies.

121.   Analyzes how professional coaching differs from traditional training.

122.   Describe how to create a training plan tailored to an organization's needs.

123.   Explains how to promote collaborative learning in business.

124.   Analyzes the importance of feedback in continuing education.

125.   Describe how companies can develop a culture of learning.

6. Language Teaching and Multilingualism (25 prompts)

126.   Describe the benefits of bilingualism on the brain.

127.   Compare different methods of

learning foreign languages.

128.   Explains how technology makes language learning easier.

129.   Analyzes the challenges adult learners face in learning a language.

130.   Describe how language immersion accelerates language learning.

131.   Explains how to teach a foreign language effectively.

132.   Analyzes the impact of accents on foreign language communication.

133.   Describe how travel and culture influence language learning.

134.   Explains how music and movies help learn a language.

135.   Compare language learning apps like Duolingo and Babbel .

136.   Analyzes the importance of linguistic exchanges in learning a language.

137.   Describe how to improve pronunciation in a foreign language.

138.   Explain why some languages are more difficult to learn than others.

139.   Analyzes the effect of multilingualism on memory and cognition.

140.   Describe how to structure an

effective language lesson.

141.   Explains how to integrate grammar into language learning.

142.   Analyzes the impact of body language in language learning.

143.   Describe how to teach a foreign language to children.

144.   Explain why some people learn a language more quickly.

145.   Compare online and face-to-face language learning.

146.   Analyze the benefits of language stays on language progress.

147.   Describe how to overcome the fear of speaking a foreign language.

148.   Explains how translation and interpretation differ in terms of learning.

149.   Analyzes the effects of contact with native speakers on language learning.

150.   Describe how storytelling can help memorize the vocabulary of a language.

7. Inclusion and Accessibility in Education (25 prompts)

151.   Describe how to make education more inclusive for students with disabilities.

152.   Analyzes the impact of assistive technologies on the learning of students with disabilities.

153.   Explains why it is important to adapt teaching materials to students' needs.

154.   Compares the challenges of school inclusion in different countries.

155.   Describe how to effectively teach students with learning disabilities.

156.   Explains how Braille makes education easier for visually impaired people.

157.   Analyzes how schools can improve accessibility for students with special needs.

158.   Describe how to adapt exams for students with disabilities.

159.   Explains how to foster an equitable learning environment.

160.   Analyzes the challenges of teaching autistic students.

161.   Describe how to train teachers in inclusive education.

162.   Explains how parents can support the learning of children who are struggling.

163.   Analyzes the impact of

school accommodations on the success of students with special needs.

164.   Describe how to use technology to improve accessibility in education.

165.   Explains how teachers can encourage acceptance and diversity in the classroom.

166.   Analyzes the differences between inclusion and integration in education.

167.   Describe how to help students with language disorders.

168.   Explains why teaching methods must be adapted to each student.

169.   neurotypical students .

170.   Describe how to teach students with attention deficit disorder.

171.   Explains how universities can improve accessibility for students with disabilities.

172.   Analyzes the benefits of an inclusive educational program for society.

173.   Describe how public policies can improve inclusive education.

174.   Explains why digital accessibility is essential for online learning.

175.   Explores how teachers can use

empathy to help struggling students.

8. Education and Sustainable Development (25 prompts)

176. Describe how to integrate education for sustainable development into school curricula.

177. Analyzes the impact of education on environmental awareness.

178. Explains why teaching responsible consumption to young people is essential.

179. Compare green initiatives in schools in different countries.

180. Describe how schools can reduce their carbon footprint.

181. Explains how teachers can encourage green practices among students.

182. Analyzes the importance of educational gardens in education for sustainable development.

183. Describe how students can get involved in sustainable development projects.

184. Explains why companies are looking for employees who are aware of sustainable development.

185.   Analyzes the effects of climate change on education in developing countries.

186.   Describe how science lessons can integrate ecological themes.

187.   Explains why environmental ethics education is important.

188.   Analyzes how schools can encourage sustainable mobility.

189.   Describe how to organize eco-friendly school events.

190.   Explains how to teach students about the circular economy.

191.   Analyzes the impact of biodiversity education on environmental protection.

192.   Describe how young people can be actors in sustainable development.

193.   Explains how to use educational games to teach ecology.

194.   Analyzes how the climate crisis influences education.

195.   Describe how to promote zero waste in schools.

196.   Explains why it is essential to teach students about the green economy.

197.   Analyzes the impact of green technologies on education.

198.   Describe how schools can use renewable energy.

199.   Explains how to raise awareness among students about global sustainable development challenges.

200.   Analyzes how education can contribute to a more sustainable future.

CHAPTER 6.MARKETING AND E-COMMERCE

Introduction: Artificial Intelligence for Marketing and E-Commerce

Artificial intelligence (AI) is revolutionizing **marketing and e-commerce** , enabling businesses to optimize their strategies, improve customer experience, and increase sales. With AI, brands can now analyze **massive amounts of data in real-time** , understand consumer preferences, and provide them with highly personalized offers.

AI also helps automate **and optimize many marketing tasks** , from creating advertising content to managing customer service. It plays a key role in improving **customer relations** , by offering smoother interactions and providing instant answers thanks to intelligent chatbots.

In this collection of **prompts dedicated to marketing and e-commerce** , we will explore several applications of AI:

- **Personalization of product recommendations** : By analyzing consumer behavior, AI can suggest products tailored to each customer's preferences, thereby increasing conversion rates.

- **Consumer Behavior Analysis** : AI helps decipher market trends and purchasing habits to refine marketing strategies.

- **Chatbots and virtual assistants for customer service** : These automated tools answer customer questions 24/7, improving customer satisfaction and reducing support costs.

- **Create targeted and optimized ads** : AI algorithms analyze user data to create relevant and effective ads.

- **Automatic generation of product descriptions** : AI can write accurate and attractive descriptions for e-commerce catalogs, optimized for SEO and conversion.

Artificial intelligence brings **a major competitive advantage to companies** by allowing them to be more responsive, more efficient and closer to their customers. **This prompts guide will help you fully exploit the potential of AI in marketing and online commerce** , in order to optimize your strategies and maximize your success.

Here are 200 prompts in the field of Marketing and Electronic Commerce , organized into several categories.

1. Digital Marketing Strategies (25 prompts)

1. Explains how to create an effective digital marketing strategy.
2. Analyzes current trends in digital marketing.
3. Compare the benefits of content marketing and paid marketing.
4. Describes how to optimize a website for SEO.
5. Explains how to use Google Ads to generate sales.
6. omnichannel marketing .
7. Describe how to use marketing automation to improve conversion.
8. Explains how to measure return on investment (ROI) in digital marketing.
9. Compare influencer marketing and traditional advertising.
10. Describe how chatbots can improve the customer experience.
11. most effective remarketing strategies .
12. Explains how to segment your audience for targeted advertising campaigns.
13. Describe the benefits of mobile marketing.
14. Compare B2B marketing and B2C marketing.
15. Explains how artificial intelligence is transforming digital marketing.

16. Analyzes the impact of social media algorithms on marketing.
17. Describe how to use storytelling in marketing.
18. Explains how to optimize a landing page to increase conversions.
19. Analyzes the role of sensory marketing in customer experience.
20. Describe how to use customer data to personalize marketing.
21. Compare online and in-store customer loyalty strategies.
22. Explains how ethical marketing influences consumer perception.
23. Analyzes the evolution of video marketing trends.
24. Describe how to succeed in a viral marketing campaign.
25. Explains why email marketing remains a powerful tool in 2025.

2. Advertising and Customer Acquisition (25 prompts)

26. Describe how to design an effective Facebook ad.
27. Compare the benefits of native advertising and display advertising.

28. Explains how to optimize an online advertising budget.

29. Analyzes the impact of programmatic advertising on digital marketing.

30. Describe how to use TikTok Ads to reach a young audience.

31. Explains why advertising on YouTube is essential for some brands.

32. Compare influencer marketing and PPC (pay -per-click).

33. Describe common mistakes to avoid in digital advertising.

34. Analyzes the impact of emotional advertising on customer loyalty.

35. Explains how to create an ad that converts.

36. Compares the performance of video ads and static ads.

37. Describes how to test and optimize advertising campaigns.

38. Explains how to use lookalike audiences on Facebook.

39. Analyzes how targeted advertising influences purchasing behaviors.

40. Describe how to use customer reviews to boost an ad.

41. Explains why short formats dominate online advertising.

42. retargeting trends in 2025.

43. Describe how to do A/B testing on an advertising campaign.

44. Explains how to use referral marketing to attract customers.

45. Compare the results of advertising campaigns on Facebook and LinkedIn.

46. Describe how to avoid advertising saturation among consumers.

47. Explains how to use audio advertising in a marketing strategy.

48. Analyzes the impact of AdBlockers on online advertising.

49. Describe how mobile advertising has evolved in recent years.

50. Explains how brands can use product placement in advertising.

3. Content Marketing and SEO (25 prompts)

51. Describe how to write an SEO-optimized article.

52. Analyze SEO trends in 2025.

53. Explains why content marketing is crucial for businesses.

54. Compare blogging and podcasting as content strategies.

55. Describe how to choose the right keywords

for an SEO strategy.

56. Explains how to structure an article for natural referencing.

57. Analyzes the impact of Google updates on SEO.

58. effective backlink strategy .

59. Explains how to optimize images for SEO.

60. form content and short-form content.

61. Describe how to use videos to improve your SEO.

62. Explains why Core Web Vitals are important for SEO.

63. Analyzes how Google EEAT influences SEO.

64. evergreen content strategy .

65. Explains how to boost organic traffic with optimized articles.

66. most popular blogging platforms .

67. Describe how to use social media to improve SEO.

68. Explains how local SEO influences local commerce.

69. Analyzes how ChatGPT and AI impact content marketing.

70. Describe how to use infographics for content marketing.

71. Explains how to create an effective editorial calendar.

72. Compare on-page and off-page SEO strategies.

73. Describe the importance of competitor analysis in SEO.

74. Explains how interactive content improves user engagement.

75. Analyzes how podcasts are influencing modern content strategies.

4. E-Commerce and Sales (25 prompts)

76. Explains how to create a profitable e-commerce store.

77. Analyzes current trends in e-commerce.

78. Describe strategies to increase the conversion rate of an e-commerce site.

79. Explains how to use dropshipping to start a business.

80. Compare Shopify , WooCommerce and Magento .

81. Describe how to optimize a product sheet to maximize sales.

82. Explains how to use affiliate marketing in e-commerce.

83. Analyzes the impact of mobile commerce on purchasing habits.

84. Describe how to manage efficient customer

service in e-commerce.

85. Explains how to improve the user experience of an e-commerce site.

86. pricing and fixed pricing strategies .

87. Describe how to build customer loyalty in an online store.

88. Explains how to reduce shopping cart abandonment rate.

89. Analyze the benefits of an e-commerce loyalty program.

90. Describe how to integrate live shopping into an e-commerce strategy.

91. Explains how to use chatbots to improve sales.

92. Compare marketplaces (Amazon, eBay, Etsy) to sell your products.

93. Describe how to successfully launch an e-commerce product.

94. Explains how to use augmented reality to improve online sales.

95. Analyzes the logistical challenges of online commerce.

96. Describe how to use influencers to boost e-commerce.

97. Explains how to optimize the loading speed of an e-commerce site.

98. Compare online and physical commerce.

99. Describe how to integrate AI into an e-

commerce site.

100.   Explains how to manage customer feedback to improve satisfaction.

5. Branding Strategies and Brand Identity (25 prompts)

101.   Describe how to create a strong, consistent brand identity.

102.   Analyzes the impact of branding on customer loyalty.

103.   Explains how storytelling strengthens brand image.

104.   successful and failed rebranding strategies .

105.   Describe how to choose an effective brand name.

106.   Explains how colors influence the perception of a brand.

107.   Analyze why certain brands become iconic.

108.   Describe how to use brand ambassadors to increase awareness.

109.   Explains how a brand can differentiate itself from the competition.

110.   Analyzes the impact of customer reviews on brand image.

111.   Describe how customer

experience shapes a brand's identity.

112. Explains why some brands use minimalism in their design.

113. Compare the pros and cons of personal vs corporate branding.

114. Describe how brands use social media to build authority.

115. Explains how authenticity influences brand perception.

116. Analyze why some brands rely on an emotional message.

117. Describe how to create an impactful and memorable slogan.

118. Explains how to measure the effectiveness of a branding strategy.

119. Compares branding strategies in luxury and mass distribution.

120. Describe how a brand can bounce back after a reputation crisis.

121. Explains why some brands choose eco-friendly branding.

122. Analyzes the role of packaging in a brand's image.

123. Describe how to use public relations to strengthen a brand.

124. Explains why some brands rely on exclusivity to attract customers.

125. Analyzes the

importance of visual consistency across different marketing media.

6. Social Networks and Influence Marketing (25 prompts)

126. Explains how to choose the right social platform for a business.

127. Analyzes why TikTok has become a powerful lever for brands.

128. Describe how to create an effective social media strategy.

129. Explains how to interact with your community on Instagram.

130. Compare the benefits of a professional and personal account on LinkedIn.

131. Describe how to boost engagement on a Facebook page.

132. Explains why social media algorithms change so often.

133. Analyzes how brands use memes to reach younger generations.

134. Describe how hashtags influence post visibility.

135. Explains how to use viral trends to your advantage.

136. Compare different types of high-performing social media posts.

137. Describe how to measure the success of a social media campaign.

138. Explains why Instagram and Facebook stories have become essential.

139. Analyzes how influencers can boost brand awareness.

140. Describe how to choose the right influencer for a collaboration.

141. Explains how to avoid fake influencers in a marketing strategy.

142. Compare the benefits of organic marketing and paid advertising on social networks.

143. Describe how to handle a crisis on social media.

144. Explains why interactive content (polls, quizzes) generates more engagement.

145. Analyzes the impact of live broadcasts on the interaction between brands and their audience.

146. Describe how a small business can benefit from social media.

147. Generated Content (UGC) marketing.

148. Compare short video formats (TikTok, Reels, YouTube Shorts).

149. Describe why some brands

choose not to be present on all networks.

150.   Explains how to optimize an Instagram bio to attract followers.

7. Email Marketing and Customer Relations (25 prompts)

151.   Explains how to write an eye-catching email subject line.

152.   Analyzes why email marketing remains effective despite the rise of social media.

153.   Describes how to segment an email list for best results.

154.   Explains how to create a successful automated email sequence.

155.   Compare email open rates across industries.

156.   Describe how to prevent your emails from ending up in spam.

157.   Explains why email design influences conversion rate.

158.   Analyzes the impact of personalized emails on customer engagement.

159.   Describe how to measure the performance of an email marketing campaign.

160.   Explains why newsletters are a

powerful loyalty tool.

161.   Compare the most popular email marketing platforms.

162.   Describes how to retrieve emails without being intrusive.

163.   Explains how companies use AB testing in email marketing.

164.   Analyzes why some email marketing campaigns fail.

165.   Describe how to write a compelling promotional email.

166.   Explains why welcome emails are essential in digital marketing.

167.   Compare the benefits of SMS marketing and email marketing.

168.   Describe how to use urgency and scarcity in a promotional email.

169.   Explains why email sending frequency impacts engagement.

170.   Analyzes how a company can automate customer relations by email.

171.   Describe how to win back a lost customer through email marketing.

172.   Explains how to integrate AI into an email marketing strategy.

173.   Compare click-through rates of emails with and without images.

174.   Describe how to use customer

testimonials in email marketing.

175. Explains how to optimize the signature of a professional email.

8. Trends and Innovations in Marketing (25 prompts)

176. Analyzes how Web3 will impact digital marketing.

177. Describe the importance of data in modern marketing strategies.

178. Explains why personalization has become a standard in marketing.

179. Compare AI-based marketing to traditional marketing.

180. Describe how NFTs are used by brands to build customer loyalty.

181. Explains why the metaverse is becoming an opportunity for marketers.

182. Analyzes the impact of new regulations on advertising tracking .

183. Describe how experiential marketing improves brand image.

184. Explains why brands are increasingly investing in audio marketing.

185. Compare the impact of influencer marketing on different generations.

186.   Describe how podcasts have become a powerful marketing tool.

187.   Explains how businesses are using marketing automation in 2025.

188.   Analyzes how 5G will transform mobile advertising strategies.

189.   Describe how voice assistants influence consumer behavior.

190.   Explains why green marketing has become a key argument.

191.   Compares the marketing strategies of large companies and startups.

192.   Describe how recommendation algorithms influence online purchases.

193.   Explains why emotion-based marketing is more effective.

194.   Analyzes the impact of new social platforms on digital advertising.

195.   Describe how brands are using gamification marketing.

196.   Explains how the attention economy influences marketing decisions.

197.   Compare digital marketing trends in 2020 vs 2025.

198.   Describe how neuromarketing influences advertising strategies.

199.   Explains how businesses can use micro-influencers.

200.   Analyzes how social
networks are evolving towards increased
monetization.

CHAPTER 7.INDUSTRY AND AUTOMATION

Introduction: Artificial Intelligence at the Service of Industry and Automation

intelligence **(AI) is revolutionizing industry and automation** , enabling companies to **gain efficiency, precision and profitability** . Thanks to technological advances, factories and production lines are becoming **smarter and more autonomous** , reducing costs, minimizing errors and optimizing processes.

AI plays a key role in **predictive maintenance, logistics optimization, quality control and industrial robotics** , transforming the way industries operate. It enables real-time data analysis, predicting failures before they occur and automating **complex tasks with unmatched precision** .

In this collection of **prompts dedicated to industry and automation** , we will explore several key applications of AI:

- **Predictive equipment maintenance** : Through real-time data analysis, AI can detect signs of failure before a breakdown occurs, preventing costly production downtime.

- **Supply Chain Optimization** : By analyzing production and distribution flows, AI improves inventory management, reduces delivery times, and optimizes routes.

- **Automated quality control** : Systems based on computer vision and machine learning help detect defects and ensure consistent quality on production lines.

- **Industrial Robotics** : AI powers collaborative robots (" cobots ") that work alongside humans, improving productivity and reducing the risk of error.

- **Optimized production planning** : By analyzing trends and demand, AI helps adjust production rates to avoid surpluses and shortages.

Artificial intelligence is redefining **the future of manufacturing** , making factories **smarter, more flexible, and more competitive** . **This prompts guide will provide you with the tools you need to harness the full potential of AI in manufacturing and automation, to improve your performance and optimize your production processes.**

Here are 200 prompts in the field of Industry and Automation .

1. Industry 4.0 and digital transformation (25 prompts)

1. Explains how Industry 4.0 is transforming manufacturing processes.
2. Analyzes the impact of digitalization on the competitiveness of industrial companies.
3. Describe how connected objects (IoT) optimize industrial production.
4. Explains how artificial intelligence is used in Industry 4.0.
5. Compare the differences between Industry 3.0 and Industry 4.0.
6. Describe how real-time data improves industrial decision-making.
7. Explains how digital twins are used for predictive maintenance.
8. Analyzes the importance of cloud computing in industrial modernization.
9. Describe how blockchain can secure industrial supply chains.
10. Explains how Manufacturing Execution Systems (MES) improve production.
11. Compare the advantages and disadvantages of smart factories.
12. Describe how automation reduces human errors in production.
13. IoT sensors help monitor the health of

machines.

14. Analyzes how big data is used to optimize production chains.

15. Describe how collaborative robots (cobots) are revolutionizing industrial work.

16. Explains how 3D printing is accelerating industrial manufacturing.

17. Compares the effectiveness of ERP systems in industrial management.

18. Describe how 5G improves connectivity in industry.

19. Explains how edge computing improves machine responsiveness.

20. Analyzes how cybersecurity is becoming a major issue in Industry 4.0.

21. Describe the challenges of adopting advanced technologies in industrial SMEs.

22. IoT platforms facilitate resource management.

23. Compares digital transformation approaches in Europe and Asia.

24. Describe how artificial intelligence can optimize industrial logistics.

25. Explains how smart grids improve the energy efficiency of factories.

2. Automation and industrial robotics (25 prompts)

26. Explains how industrial robots improve factory productivity.

27. Analyzes how robotic arms are used in automotive assembly.

28. Describe how autonomous mobile robots (AMRs) optimize internal logistics.

29. Explains how cobots assist human workers in production.

30. Compare the advantages of fixed and mobile robots in industry.

31. Describe how machine vision enables robots to better detect defects.

32. Explains how robots adapt to complex production tasks.

33. Analyzes how predictive maintenance prevents breakdowns of industrial robots.

34. Describe how robots reduce waste of raw materials.

35. Explains how AI improves the programming of industrial robots.

36. Compares major industrial robot manufacturers (Fanuc , ABB, KUKA, etc.).

37. Describe how robots are used in pharmaceutical production.

38. Explains how SCADA systems are used to monitor industrial robots.

39. Analyzes the challenges of integrating robots into traditional factories.

40. Describe how humanoid robots are tested in the industrial sector.

41. Explains how AI enables robots to learn in real time.

42. Compare the differences between rigid robotics and soft robotics.

43. Describe how force sensors help robots better interact with the environment.

44. Explains how machine learning improves the accuracy of robots.

45. Analyzes how robots reduce fatigue in industrial workers.

46. Describe how robots help in semiconductor production.

47. Explains how robotics influences employment in the industrial sector.

48. Compares the control systems used to drive industrial robots.

49. Describe how warehouse automation improves inventory management.

50. Explains how drones are used in monitoring industrial facilities.

3. Industrial maintenance and process optimization (25 prompts)

51. Explains how predictive maintenance improves machine availability.

52. IoT sensors detect anomalies in industrial equipment.

53. Describe how AI algorithms predict machine failures.

54. Explains how augmented reality helps maintenance technicians.

55. Compare corrective maintenance and preventive maintenance in industry.

56. Describe how automating quality testing reduces manufacturing defects.

57. Explains how real-time monitoring systems optimize factories.

58. Analyzes how optimizing production flows reduces manufacturing costs.

59. Describe how industrial energy management systems reduce consumption.

60. Explains how industrial waste management is optimized with AI.

61. Compare computerized maintenance management software (CMMS).

62. Describe how predictive maintenance improves energy efficiency.

63. Explains how smart factories adapt their production based on demand.

64. Analyzes how AI can improve the design of industrial processes.

65. Describe how inspection robots avoid risks to humans.

66. Explains how automation systems reduce human error.
67. Compares Lean and Six Sigma strategies in industrial optimization.
68. Describe how industrial simulation software helps predict production.
69. Explains how artificial intelligence optimizes supply chain management.
70. Analyzes how data analytics improves industrial equipment management.
71. Describe how exoskeletons assist factory workers.
72. IoT devices help in industrial inventory management.
73. Compare the different predictive maintenance methods.
74. Describe how autonomous vehicles facilitate the internal transportation of goods.
75. Explains how numerical modeling helps predict equipment wear.

4. Energy and sustainable development in industry (25 prompts)

76. Explains how Industry 4.0 reduces the carbon footprint of factories.

77. Analyzes how renewable energy is integrated into industrial sites.

78. Describe how resource optimization enables greener production.

79. Explains how smart grids improve industrial energy efficiency.

80. Compare energy saving solutions in modern factories.

81. Describe how material recycling is optimized with AI.

82. Explains how automation helps reduce industrial waste.

83. Analyzes how companies are adopting sustainable manufacturing practices.

84. Describe how intelligent resource management optimizes industry.

85. Explains how using sensors can reduce water consumption.

86. Compare the environmental challenges between heavy industry and high-tech industry.

87. Describe how environmental regulations influence industrial practices.

88. Explains how AI can improve the energy efficiency of machines.

89. Analyzes how alternative energies are adopted by industry.

90. Describe how zero carbon factories are

designed.

5. Safety and industrial risk management (25 prompts)

91. Explains how AI helps detect anomalies in industrial processes.
92. Analyzes how cybersecurity protects connected industrial systems.
93. Describe how safety protocols are being strengthened in Factories 4.0.
94. Explains how virtual reality is used for industrial safety training.
95. Compare the benefits of smart safety sensors in industry.
96. Describe how SCADA systems are protected against cyber attacks.
97. Explains how industrial risk management is optimized with AI.
98. Analyzes how automation improves worker safety in factories.
99. Describe how drone inspections improve facility monitoring.

100. Explains how incident management systems reduce production downtime.

101. Compare ISO standards for industrial safety.

102.	Describe how augmented reality training improves emergency preparedness.

103.	Explains how chemicals are managed safely in factories.

104.	Analyzes how industrial companies minimize accident risks.

105.	Describe how blockchain can secure industrial transactions.

106.	IoT sensors improve gas leak detection.

107.	Compares safety protocols of industrial robots and humans.

108.	Describe how data analysis helps anticipate industrial incidents.

109.	Explains how connected protective equipment improves safety.

110.	Analyzes how robotics can be used for interventions in hazardous environments.

111.	Describe how early warning systems work in industrial sites.

112.	Explains how digital simulations help in disaster prevention.

113.	Compares fire detection technologies in industrial sites.

114.	Describe how security audits are automated with artificial intelligence.

115.   Explains how industrial voice assistants improve emergency responsiveness.

6. Logistics and Supply Chain Management (25 prompts)

116.   Explains how AI optimizes industrial inventory management.

117.   Analyzes how blockchain improves the traceability of industrial products.

118.   Describe how autonomous vehicles make it easier to transport goods.

119.   IoT sensors improve warehouse management.

120.   Compare the benefits of automated storage in modern factories.

121.   Describe how ERP systems facilitate industrial supplier management.

122.   Explains how data analytics improves logistics route optimization.

123.   Analyzes how autonomous robots reduce delivery times.

124.   Describe how companies are using RFID to track industrial materials.

125.   Explains how artificial intelligence predicts fluctuations in demand.

126.	Compare intelligent transportation solutions in the industrial sector.

127.	Describe how raw materials management is optimized with machine learning.

128.	Explains how drones are used to monitor industrial warehouses.

129.	Analyzes how logistics information systems reduce human errors.

130.	Describe how optimization algorithms improve industrial supply.

131.	Explains how just-in-time flows are managed with advanced technologies.

132.	Compare green logistics strategies to reduce carbon footprint.

133.	Describe how predictive maintenance reduces logistics disruptions.

134.	Explains how electric vehicles are transforming industrial logistics.

135.	Analyzes how AI is used to negotiate transportation rates.

136.	Describe how virtual assistants improve industrial order management.

137.	Explains how sales forecasts influence logistics strategies.

138. Compare traditional and automated warehouse management systems.

139. Describe how cloud solutions improve logistics collaboration.

140. supply platforms chain optimizes industrial purchases.

7. Artificial intelligence and industrial innovation (25 prompts)

141. Explains how deep learning is used in manufacturing defect recognition.

142. Analyzes how AI can optimize industrial production in real time.

143. Describe how natural language processing is applied to industrial maintenance.

144. Explains how machine learning improves resource management.

145. Compares optimization algorithms used in smart factories.

146. Describe how AI assistants help industrial engineers.

147. Explains how AI is used to personalize on-demand production.

148. Analyzes how artificial intelligence improves failure management.

149.   Describe how AI technologies help automate administrative tasks in factories.

150.   Explains how predictive models are used to anticipate energy needs.

151.   Compare the different applications of computer vision in industry.

152.   Describe how AI improves industrial product design.

153.   Explains how reinforcement learning is used to optimize production.

154.   Analyzes how voice recognition helps industrial operators.

155.   Describe how AI is helping improve safety in chemical plants.

156.   Explains how industrial chatbots facilitate human resources management.

157.   Compare AI tools used for real-time machine management.

158.   Describe how expert systems assist industrial engineers.

159.   Explains how AI is used to automate quality control testing.

160.   Analyzes how AI technologies are transforming advanced manufacturing processes.

161. Describe how companies are using AI to monitor working conditions.

162. Explains how supervised learning algorithms improve maintenance.

163. Compare AI models used to optimize energy consumption in factories.

164. Describe how virtual assistants facilitate the supervision of industrial sites.

165. Explains how neural networks improve industrial simulations.

8. Future of Industry and new trends (25 prompts)

166. Explains how industrial companies adapt to new technologies.

167. Analyzes how distributed manufacturing will transform the industry.

168. Describe how Industry 5.0 will further integrate humans into production.

169. Explains how smart cities will influence the industries of the future.

170. Compares sustainable industrial development strategies on a global scale.

171. Describe how smart materials research will impact manufacturing.

172.   Explains how the merger between biotechnology and industry will evolve.

173.   Analyzes how biological robots could replace certain machines.

174.   Describe how 4D printing could revolutionize industrial production.

175.   Explains how smart waste management could transform the industry.

176.   Compares investments in industrial AI between major economic powers.

177.   Describe how Industry 5.0 could create more skilled jobs.

178.   Explains how the circular economy could fit into manufacturing.

179.   Analyzes how the evolution of batteries could impact heavy industries.

180.   Describe how deep tech startups are revolutionizing the industry.

181.   Explains how the convergence between quantum and industry could work.

182.   Analyzes how nuclear fusion could power the factories of the future.

183.   Describe how cognitive robotics could change factories.

184.   Explains how 6G networks will impact the industry.

185.   Analyze how space factories could come into being.

186-200. [Add any emerging trends as needed]

9. Emerging technologies and disruptive innovations in industry

186.   Explains how 3D printing systems are moving towards more sustainable materials.

187.   Analyzes how quantum computing could accelerate industrial optimization.

188.   Describe how the fusion of AI and humanoid robotics could improve factories.

189.   Explains how the hydrogen economy could transform manufacturing.

190.   Compares sustainability initiatives in the automotive and aerospace industries.

191.   Describe how solid-state batteries could impact the energy industry.

192.   Explains how biotechnologies influence tomorrow's

industrial production.

193.		Analyzes how collaborative robotics could make factories more flexible.

194.		Describe how decentralized manufacturing could reduce production costs.

195.		Explains how telepresence and the metaverse can be used in the factories of the future.

196.		Compare the benefits of industrial exoskeletons for workers and technicians.

197.		Describe how nanorobots could revolutionize machine maintenance.

198.		Explains how generative AI could design optimized production lines.

199.		Analyzes how automated mining could evolve in the coming decades.

200.		Describe how brain-machine interfaces could improve industrial control.

CHAPTER 8.TRANSPORT AND MOBILITY

Introduction: Artificial Intelligence in the Service of Transport and Mobility

Artificial intelligence (AI) is profoundly transforming the **transport and mobility sector** , making travel more **efficient, safe and sustainable** . Thanks to technological advances, AI can improve traffic management, optimize routes, anticipate incidents and even drive vehicles autonomously.

AI-based solutions are revolutionizing both **individual** and **collective transport** , as well as logistics and deliveries. They enable **intelligent management of road and rail infrastructure** , while helping to reduce the carbon footprint through better planning of journeys and resources.

In this collection of **prompts dedicated to transportation and mobility** , we will explore several major applications of AI:

- **Autonomous vehicles (Tesla, Waymo, etc.)** : AI plays a central role in the development of driverless cars, allowing them to analyze their environment and make decisions in real time.

- **Traffic Optimization and Transportation Management** : Analyzing traffic data helps smooth traffic flow, reduce congestion, and improve the efficiency of public transportation.

- **Intelligent navigation systems** : Thanks to AI, GPS and mobility applications offer optimized routes based on traffic conditions and user preferences.

- **Predictive analysis of road incidents** : By relying on historical and real-time data, AI makes it possible to anticipate accidents and alert drivers or the competent authorities.

- **Automation of logistics and deliveries** : AI optimizes warehouse management, plans delivery vehicle routes and improves shipping speed.

AI is paving the way for a **smarter, smoother, and safer future of transportation** . **This prompt guide will help you fully exploit the potential of AI in mobility, in order to innovate and optimize tomorrow's transportation solutions.**

Here are 200 prompts in the field of Transportation and Mobility , covering various aspects such as technological innovations, environmental impact, logistics and future trends.

1. Innovations and technologies in transport

1. Describe the impact of autonomous vehicles on urban mobility.
2. Explains how artificial intelligence improves traffic management.
3. Analyzes the evolution of batteries for electric vehicles and their performance.
4. How could drones revolutionize freight transport?
5. Presents the technical challenges of developing hyperloops .
6. Describe the impact of 5G on connected transportation.
7. How do smart sensors improve the safety of transport infrastructure?
8. Compare the advantages and disadvantages of hydrogen and electric cars.
9. Explains how intelligent transportation systems (ITS) optimize journeys.
10. Describe how autonomous delivery robots are changing urban logistics.

2. Sustainable mobility and ecology

11. Compare policies to reduce CO_2 emissions in transport.

12. How can cities promote soft mobility such as cycling and walking?

13. Explains how biofuels can reduce the carbon footprint of air travel.

14. Analyzes the role of hydrogen trains in the future of rail.

15. What are the challenges of recycling electric car batteries?

16. Describe innovations in alternative fuels for freight trucks.

17. How do smart cities integrate sustainable transport solutions?

18. Presents the environmental impacts of manufacturing electric vehicles.

19. What are the advantages of electric and hydrogen buses for public transport?

20. How can the circular economy be applied to transport infrastructure?

3. Logistics and transport of goods

21. Describe the evolution of maritime transport towards more ecological solutions.

22. How does blockchain optimize supply chain management?

23. What are the challenges of automating

seaports?

24. Analyzes the impact of e-commerce on freight transport.

25. How are smart warehouses transforming logistics?

26. Presents the challenges of refrigerated transport in terms of energy consumption.

27. What are the advantages of autonomous freight trains?

28. Explains how big data optimizes logistics routes.

29. Describe how AI reduces costs in freight transportation management.

30. What are the challenges of the last mile in urban logistics?

4. Urban planning and transport infrastructure

31. How should urban infrastructure adapt to electric vehicles?

32. Describe new trends in the design of train stations and airports.

33. How can smart motorways improve traffic flow?

34. What are the advantages of electronic tolls for smoothing traffic flow?

35. Explains how smart parking reduces urban congestion.

36. How can sustainable construction improve transport infrastructure?

37. Describe innovations in bridge and tunnel management.

38. How do automated metro projects optimize public transport?

39. What are the challenges of expanding tram networks in cities?

40. How do new multimodal stations facilitate urban mobility?

5. Public transport and shared mobility

41. What are the benefits of shared vehicles on the urban environment?

42. Describe how multimodal subscriptions improve the user experience.

43. Analyzes the economic challenges of free public transportation.

44. How are mobile applications revolutionizing urban travel?

45. What are the challenges of maintaining electric bus fleets?

46. Describe the new trends in carpooling and car sharing.

47. How does AI integration optimize public transport routes?

48. Explains the benefits of high-speed trains

for intercity mobility.

49. What are the impacts of the development of autonomous taxis?

50. Analyzes the economic models of self-service scooters and bicycles.

6. Air and space transport

51. will electric and hybrid aircraft transform aviation?

52. What are the challenges of developing hydrogen aviation?

53. Describe the impact of space tourism on the environment.

54. How does AI help optimize air traffic control?

55. Presents innovations in aircraft noise reduction.

56. What are the advantages of new generations of supersonic aircraft?

57. How do biofuels reduce the carbon footprint of air travel?

58. Analyzes the future of flying taxis and eVTOLs .

59. How are drones revolutionizing air parcel transport?

60. What are the economic impacts of new low-cost airlines?

7. Safety and regulation of transport

61. How do new cybersecurity standards affect connected vehicles?

62. What are the challenges of regulating autonomous vehicles?

63. How does smart video surveillance improve security in public transport?

64. Explains how AI reduces road accidents.

65. What are the impacts of radars and automatic speed limitation systems?

66. How are drones used to monitor road traffic?

67. Analyzes the risks of cyberattacks on connected transport systems.

68. What are the benefits of simulators for pilot and driver training?

69. How does smart signaling reduce traffic jams?

70. What are the impacts of the new regulations on maritime transport?

8. Future of transportation and emerging trends

71. How could the Hyper Loop transform long-distance travel?

72. Describe the challenges of underwater passenger transportation.

73. What are the challenges of developing solar roads?

74. How could space elevators revolutionize space exploration?

75. What are the impacts of autonomous flying taxis on urban mobility?

76. Describe the future of amphibious vehicles in major cities.

77. How could nuclear fusion power the transportation of the future?

78. What are the challenges of developing fully autonomous cars?

79. Analyzes the prospects of magnetic supersonic trains.

80. How could AI create fully autonomous and intelligent transportation solutions?

9. Economic and social impact of transport

81. How does transport influence the economic development of regions?

82. What are the hidden costs of urban transport for municipalities?

83. Analyzes the impact of transport infrastructure on local employment.

84. What are the effects of transport strikes on a country's economy?

85. How are new transportation technologies changing the job market?

86. What are the economic issues of the privatization of transport networks?

87. How does transportation influence urban property prices?

88. Describe the impacts of government subsidies on public transportation.

89. How does the development of public transport affect worker productivity?

90. What are the economic challenges of large infrastructures such as TGV lines?

10. Tourism and transport

91. What are the effects of tourism on transport infrastructure?

92. How has air transport influenced the growth of international tourism?

93. Describe cruise trends in maritime transportation.

94. What are the challenges of tourist transport in large cities?

95. How is luxury transportation (private jets, yachts) evolving?

96. Analyzes the impact of low-cost on mass tourism.

97. How do mobility services influence the traveler experience?

98. What are the effects of transport restrictions on the tourism industry?

99. Describe innovations in eco-friendly tourist transportation.

100. How has the pandemic transformed transportation in the tourism sector?

11. Maritime and river transport

101. How does port modernization improve maritime logistics?

102. What are the challenges of the ecological transition for transport vessels?

103. Describe the impact of autonomous cargo ships on the maritime industry.

104. How does ocean management influence maritime transport?

105. What are the advantages of new fuels for ships?

106. How are rivers and canals used for transporting goods?

107. Describe the changes in regulations in maritime transport.

108. What are the risks of storms and natural disasters on sea transport?

109. How AI and smart sensors improve maritime navigation?

110. Analyzes the logistical challenges of maritime transport in the Arctic.

12. Accessibility and inclusion in transport

111. How to make public transport more accessible to people with disabilities?

112. What are the mobility challenges for seniors in urban areas?

113. Describe innovations that facilitate accessibility in train stations and airports.

114. How does digital technology help people with disabilities to move around better?

115. What are the impacts of free transport for low-income people?

116. How to adapt transport to the needs of children and families?

117. What are the challenges of inclusive mobility in rural areas?

118. How do smart cities integrate accessibility solutions?

119. What are the benefits of wheelchair accessible transport?

120. How can urban planning promote inclusive mobility?

13. Security and risk management

121.   How does facial recognition improve transportation security?

122.   What are the risks associated with connected and autonomous vehicles?

123.   How is cybersecurity applied in the transportation sector?

124.   What are the challenges of managing natural disasters on transport infrastructure?

125.   How do simulations help improve transportation safety?

126.   Describe innovations in rail accident prevention.

127.   How do airlines handle crises and emergencies?

128.   What are the effects of radars and speed checks on road safety?

129.   How can transport infrastructure be protected against terrorism?

130.   What are the impacts of alcohol and drugs on road safety?

14. Rural mobility and isolated infrastructure

131.   What are the challenges of

transport in rural areas?

132.　　　　　How can drones facilitate transportation in isolated environments?

133.　　　　　What are the impacts of unmaintained roads on rural communities?

134.　　　　　Describe the importance of small stations and branch railway lines.

135.　　　　　How can public transport be improved in rural areas?

136.　　　　　What are the benefits of electric vehicles for isolated villages?

137.　　　　　How can governments better finance rural infrastructure?

138.　　　　　What are the logistics challenges of delivering goods in the countryside?

139.　　　　　Describe innovative solutions for transportation in remote areas.

140.　　　　　How does teleworking influence rural mobility?

15. Vehicles of the future and new mobility

141.　　　　How could flying cars transform the way we travel?

142.　　　　What are the impacts of the transition to 100% autonomous vehicles?

143.　　　　Describe the trends in electric and eco-friendly motorcycles.

144.　　　　How is robotics used in the development of new vehicles?

145.　　　　What are the challenges of wireless charging of electric vehicles?

146.　　　　How do smart tires improve transportation safety?

147.　　　　What are the new vehicle designs to optimize energy consumption?

148.　　　　Describe the use of nanotechnology in transportation.

149.　　　　How is AI-powered vehicle customization changing the industry?

150.　　　　What are the impacts of exoskeletons on the mobility of people with reduced mobility?

16. Rail transport and innovations

151.　　　　How can autonomous trains revolutionize rail transport?

152.　　　　What are the advantages of new materials used in rails and wagons?

153.　　　　How does high speed affect intercity transport?

154.　　　　What are the challenges of modernizing old railway networks?

155.　　　　How do solar and hybrid trains

reduce carbon footprint?

156.   What are the impacts of the development of the magnetic levitation train?

157.   How do smart stations improve passenger experience?

158.   What are the impacts of rail strikes on the local economy?

159.   How do hybrid trains combine hydrogen and electricity?

160.   What are the new economic models of railway companies?

17. Space transportation and the future of interplanetary mobility

161.   How will space tourism evolve in the next 50 years?

162.   What are the challenges of transporting goods in space?

163.   How will lunar bases influence future transportation systems?

164.   Describe the transportation challenges of colonizing Mars.

165.   What are the advantages of reusable space shuttles?

166.   How could nuclear-powered rockets revolutionize space exploration?

167.   What are the impacts of

the development of the commercial space station?

168.   How will robots and AI be used for space logistics?

169.   What are the challenges of transporting water and oxygen in space?

170.   How could artificial gravity improve space transportation?

18. Transportation and artificial intelligence

171.   How does artificial intelligence optimize road traffic management?

172.   What are the benefits of AI-based driving assistants?

173.   How do machine learning algorithms improve transportation forecasting?

174.   Describe the impacts of AI on public transportation optimization.

175.   How does computer vision help in detecting road hazards?

19. Political and legislative issues of transport

176.   What are the main legislative challenges of autonomous vehicles?

177.   How are governments regulating the rise of self-service scooters and bikes?

178.   Describe the implications of carbon taxes on transportation companies.

179.   How are sustainable mobility policies implemented globally?

180.   What are the challenges of privatizing public transport infrastructure?

20. Transport and big data

181.   How does big data help predict passenger flows in transport?

182.   What are the benefits of smart sensors for improving transportation efficiency?

183.   How do cities use data to improve traffic flow?

184.   Describe the use of heat maps to optimize public transportation routes.

185.   How does real-time data improve airport and train station management?

21. Transport and blockchain

186.   How can blockchain secure

transportation transactions?

187.   What are the benefits of blockchain for supply chain management?

188.   How can smart contracts facilitate the management of freight transport?

189.   Describe the application of blockchain in autonomous vehicle tracking.

190.   What are the potential impacts of cryptocurrencies on the transportation industry?

22. Psychology and sociology of transport

191.   How does the choice of transport modes influence individuals' well-being?

192.   What are the psychological effects of long commutes on workers?

193.   How does culture influence the adoption of new modes of transportation?

194.   Describe user behaviors in the face of service delays and interruptions.

195.   How do transportation networks influence social interactions in cities?

23. Transport and natural disasters

196.   How can transport infrastructure be adapted to natural disasters?

197.   What are the challenges of transportation during humanitarian crises?

198.   How do airports and train stations prepare for natural disasters?

199.   Describe innovations in emergency transportation during disasters.

200.   What are the impacts of extreme weather events on global logistics?

CHAPTER 9. AGRICULTURE AND THE ENVIRONMENT

Introduction: Artificial Intelligence in the Service of Agriculture and the Environment

Faced with the challenges of **climate change, food security and sustainable resource management** , artificial intelligence (AI) is proving to be a major asset for agriculture **and environmental protection** . Thanks to technological advances, it is now possible to **optimize agricultural practices, improve natural resource management and minimize the environmental impact of human activities** .

AI enables farmers and environmental experts to analyze **complex data in real time** , anticipate climate variations and make more informed decisions. It thus contributes to more **precise, productive and sustainable agriculture** , while helping to preserve **ecosystems and biodiversity** .

In this collection of **prompts dedicated to agriculture and the environment** , we will explore several major applications of AI:

- **Crop monitoring and disease detection** : Through the analysis of satellite and drone images, AI can quickly identify signs of disease or water stress in crops.

- **Optimization of irrigation and natural resources** : AI helps manage water efficiently by adapting irrigation to the actual needs of plants, thus reducing waste.

- **Weather prediction** : Machine learning analyzes climate models to anticipate extreme events and help farmers better plan their operations.

- **Soil analysis and yield optimization** : By assessing soil quality and recommending suitable strategies, AI improves productivity while preserving agricultural land.

- **Waste management and automated sorting** : AI facilitates the sorting and recycling of waste by automating its recognition and classification, thus contributing to better resource management.

Thanks to AI, we now have the opportunity to **reinvent agriculture and environmental protection** , adopting **smarter and more sustainable solutions** . **This prompts guide will help you explore and leverage these technologies to shape a greener and more efficient future.**

Here are 200 prompts in the field of Agriculture and the Environment , organized by theme.

1. Agriculture and technology

1. How is artificial intelligence transforming modern agriculture?
2. What are the benefits of agricultural drones for crop monitoring?
3. How does IoT (Internet of Things) help optimize agricultural production?
4. What are the impacts of robotization on the work of farmers?
5. How do smart sensors improve irrigation management?
6. How can biotechnology revolutionize agriculture?
7. How does farm management software improve yields?
8. What are the ethical issues related to the use of GMOs?
9. How can blockchain improve the traceability of agricultural products?
10. How could 3D printing be used in agriculture?

2. Sustainable agriculture and permaculture

11. What are the fundamental principles of permaculture?
12. How can intercropping improve

agricultural productivity?

13. What are the benefits of composting for farms?

14. How does organic farming differ from conventional farming?

15. What are the challenges of developing urban agriculture?

16. How to reduce the use of pesticides in agriculture?

17. What are the benefits of agroforestry for biodiversity?

18. How can natural fertilizers replace chemical fertilizers?

19. What are the advantages and disadvantages of hydroponics?

20. How can microfarms contribute to food security?

3. Climate and environmental impact

21. What are the impacts of climate change on agriculture?

22. How can agriculture reduce its carbon footprint?

23. How can regenerative agricultural practices restore soils?

24. How to combat the desertification of agricultural land?

25. What are the effects of intensive agriculture

on ecosystems?

26. How can forests help combat global warming?

27. What are the challenges of reforestation and reforestation?

28. How does plastic pollution threaten agricultural land?

29. How can nature-based solutions help climate adaptation?

30. What are the effects of soil erosion on agricultural productivity?

4. Water and resource management

31. How to optimize water management on farms?

32. What are the impacts of excessive irrigation on the environment?

33. How can rainwater harvesting be integrated into agriculture?

34. What are the issues surrounding groundwater pollution from agriculture?

35. How can seawater desalination be a solution for irrigation?

36. How can modern technologies help reduce water waste?

37. What are the advantages of drip irrigation systems?

38. How can wetlands be protected from

agricultural activities?

39. What are the impacts of climate change on water resources?

40. How to raise awareness among farmers about saving water?

5. Biodiversity and agricultural ecosystems

41. Why is biodiversity essential to agriculture?

42. How do pollinators influence agricultural production?

43. What are the dangers of bee decline on food production?

44. How to promote biodiversity on farms?

45. What are the effects of monoculture on soil health?

46. How to preserve plant species threatened by intensive agriculture?

47. How can hedgerows and meadows benefit biodiversity?

48. What are the roles of earthworms in agriculture?

49. How to combat invasive species in agricultural crops?

50. How does crop rotation contribute to soil preservation?

6. Innovation and the future of

agriculture

51. What are the challenges of food production for a growing world population?

52. How could artificial intelligence predict agricultural yields?

53. How could synthetic biology transform agriculture?

54. What are the advantages and limitations of vertical farms?

55. How can lab-grown meat production impact the environment?

56. What are the challenges of genetic editing in agricultural crops?

57. How do satellites help monitor agricultural yields?

58. How can mushrooms play a role in sustainable agriculture?

59. How could nanotechnology be applied to agriculture?

60. What are the impacts of artificial intelligence on farm management?

7. Food and responsible consumption

61. How can we encourage the consumption of local and seasonal products?

62. What are the environmental impacts of industrial farming?

63. How to encourage the reduction of food waste?

64. What are the benefits of a low environmental impact diet?

65. How do organic labels guarantee better sustainability?

66. How can we raise consumer awareness of the impact of their diet?

67. What are the effects of intensive agriculture on the nutritional quality of food?

68. How do short circuits contribute to the ecological transition?

69. What are the challenges facing agriculture in the face of increasing demand for plant proteins?

70. How can transparency in the food supply chain be improved?

8. Agricultural waste management and recycling

71. How to sustainably manage agricultural waste?

72. What are the impacts of chemical fertilizers on the environment?

73. How can methanization be a solution to agricultural waste?

74. How to recover crop residues and agricultural by-products?

75. What are the effects of microplastics on agricultural soils?

76. How to encourage the recycling of agricultural plastics?

77. What are the dangers of pesticides for soils and biodiversity?

78. How can farmers reduce their waste production?

79. How can the circular economy be applied to agriculture?

80. What are the benefits of large-scale composting for agriculture?

9. Renewable energy and agriculture

91. How can solar energy be used in agriculture?

92. What are the advantages of greenhouses heated using renewable energy?

93. How can biofuels be a solution for sustainable agriculture?

94. How to integrate wind power into agricultural operations?

95. What are the advantages of agrophotovoltaics ?

96. How can farms reduce their dependence on fossil fuels?

97. What are the challenges of energy storage

for autonomous farms?

98. How can geothermal energy be used in agriculture?

99. What are the challenges of electrifying agricultural machinery?

100. How does agricultural methanization contribute to the energy transition?

10. Agriculture and artificial intelligence

101. What are the benefits of smart sensors for monitoring crop health?

102. How can AI algorithms predict plant diseases?

103. How does AI help in selecting the best crop varieties?

104. How are agricultural robots changing farmers' work?

105. What are the benefits of weather prediction models for agriculture?

106. How can AI help optimize agricultural logistics?

107. What are the benefits of image recognition systems for identifying pests?

108. How can machine learning improve agricultural yields?

109. How is satellite data used to

monitor farms?

110. What are the challenges of collecting and analyzing agricultural data?

11. Agricultural policies and regulations

111. What are the impacts of agricultural policies on the environment?

112. How do agricultural subsidies influence food production?

113. What are the challenges of international trade for local farmers?

114. How do environmental regulations affect agriculture?

115. Why are organic farming standards important?

116. What are the challenges of the ecological transition for farmers?

117. How can governments encourage sustainable agriculture?

118. What are the effects of free trade agreements on agriculture?

119. How do pesticide use laws affect agricultural production?

120. How is the CAP (Common Agricultural Policy) evolving in the face of climate challenges?

12. Agricultural innovations for the

future

121.   What are the impacts of new drought-resistant seed varieties?

122.   How can agricultural robotics improve farm productivity?

123.   How are biopesticides an alternative to chemical pesticides?

124.   What are the challenges of developing crops in arid environments?

125.   How could plant genetics revolutionize agriculture?

126.   What are the advantages and limitations of new generation organic fertilizers?

127.   How do nanosatellites help monitor crop growth?

128.   What are the impacts of new soil conservation practices?

129.   How do autonomous drones improve the management of large farms?

130.   agroecological innovation ?

13. Social impact of agriculture

131.   How can agriculture help reduce global poverty?

132.   What are the challenges of agricultural work in developing countries?

133.   How can agricultural cooperatives improve conditions for farmers?

134.   What are the impacts of child labor in agriculture?

135.   How do microfinance programs help farmers grow?

136.   How to ensure fair remuneration for small agricultural producers?

137.   What are the challenges of the feminization of the agricultural sector?

138.   How can we promote young people's access to agricultural professions?

139.   What are the challenges of transferring farms to new generations?

140.   How can we raise awareness among the population about the realities of the agricultural world?

14. Urban agriculture and short circuits

141.   How do urban vegetable gardens contribute to food security?

142.   What are the advantages of vertical farms in urban areas?

143.   How can shared gardens boost neighborhoods?

144.   What are the benefits of AMAP (Associations for the Maintenance of Peasant Agriculture)?

145.   How to encourage restaurants to source locally?

146.   What are the challenges of short food supply chain logistics?

147.   How can supermarkets support local producers?

148.   What are the economic impacts of farmers' markets on cities?

149.   How do online sales platforms help local farmers?

150.   How can consumers better identify local products?

15. Food security and access to nutrition

151.   How can we guarantee access to quality food for all?

152.   What are the impacts of food waste on global food security?

153.   How are food banks adapting to new agricultural challenges?

154.   How do sustainable agricultural practices influence food quality?

155.   What are the roles of NGOs in the fight against malnutrition?

156.   How to improve food distribution in the event of a crisis?

157.   What are the effects of climate change on food availability?

158.   How can nutrition education influence eating habits?

159.   How to limit agricultural losses to ensure better food security?

160.   What are the challenges of producing alternative proteins (insects, algae, etc.)?

16.   Soil management and reforestation

161.   How to restore soils degraded by intensive agriculture?

162.   What are the benefits of mulching for soil preservation?

163.   How do soil conservation techniques help combat erosion?

164.   How can forests be integrated into agricultural operations?

165.   What are the effects of deforestation on agricultural biodiversity?

166.   How to reforest agricultural land while maintaining its productivity?

167.   What are the benefits of green manures for soil fertility?

168.   How to reduce soil compaction caused by the passage of agricultural machinery?

169.   How does conservation agriculture help preserve agricultural land?

170.   What are the roles of soil microorganisms in the fertility of agricultural land?

17. Biodiversity and environmental protection

171.   How to promote biodiversity on farms?

172.   What are the effects of monocultures on ecological balance?

173.   How do hedges and flower strips contribute to the preservation of wildlife?

174.   What are the impacts of pesticides on pollinators like bees?

175.   How can farmers combat soil depletion?

176.   What are the benefits of agroecological practices on biodiversity?

177.   How can crop diversification improve farm resilience?

178.   How to protect endangered

species in agricultural areas?

179.　　　What are the roles of wetlands in regulating agricultural ecosystems?

180.　　　How can farmers participate in reforestation?

18. Water resources management

181.　　　How to reduce water consumption in agriculture?

182.　　　What are the advantages of drip irrigation?

183.　　　How can artificial water reservoirs be a sustainable solution?

184.　　　How to avoid pollution of groundwater by fertilizers and pesticides?

185.　　　What are the impacts of climate change on water availability for agriculture?

186.　　　How to recycle wastewater for agricultural irrigation?

187.　　　How is hydroponic growing a sustainable alternative?

188.　　　What are the advantages and limitations of desalination for agriculture?

189.　　　How to improve watershed management for better water sharing?

190.　　　Why is adopting drought-resistant crops essential?

19. Innovations and the future of agriculture

191.   How could vertical farming meet global food needs?

192.   What are the roles of blockchain in the traceability of agricultural products?

193.   How can gene editing (CRISPR) improve agricultural productivity?

194.   How do natural biostimulants replace chemical fertilizers?

195.   What are the challenges of adopting autonomous and robotic farms?

196.   How could 3D printing food impact agriculture?

197.   What are the challenges of developing laboratory-grown meat?

198.   How could underwater farms be a solution for the future?

199.   How can the fusion of AI and plant biology transform agriculture?

200.   What are the potential impacts of nanotechnologies on sustainable agriculture?

CHAPTER 10.LAW AND SECURITY

Introduction: Artificial Intelligence in the Service of Law and Security

In a world where **legal regulation and security** are becoming increasingly complex, artificial intelligence (AI) is positioning itself as a powerful tool to **automate, analyze and strengthen decision-making** in these areas. Whether to assist legal professionals or improve risk monitoring and prevention, AI can accelerate processes and optimize the efficiency of judicial and security systems.

AI offers **advanced solutions to analyze massive volumes of legal data, detect fraud and prevent threats** , while ensuring an ethical and legally compliant framework. Its use extends to **courts, law firms, businesses, law enforcement and security agencies** .

In this collection of **prompts dedicated to law and security** , we will explore several major applications of AI:

- **Automatic analysis of contracts and legal documents** : AI facilitates the reading and interpretation of legal texts, identifying important clauses and detecting potential risks.

- **Fraud and regulatory violation detection** : AI algorithms can monitor suspicious transactions and behavior to identify financial fraud or regulatory violations.

- **Surveillance and facial recognition** : Used in public and private security, AI can identify individuals in real time, improve infrastructure security and prevent criminal acts.

- **Crime Prediction and Risk Management** : Through the analysis of criminal data and trends, AI helps authorities anticipate crimes and allocate security resources efficiently.

- **Judicial decision support** : AI assists judges and lawyers by providing case law analysis, evaluating cases, and offering recommendations based on legal precedents.

AI thus paves the way for **faster and more accessible justice, as well as enhanced security** , by reducing human error and improving prevention and intervention capacity. **This prompts guide will allow you to explore these innovations and fully exploit the potential of AI in the field of law and security.**

Here are 200 prompts in the field of Law and Security , divided into several categories.

1. Constitutional Law and Institutions

1. What are the main sources of constitutional law?
2. How does the separation of powers work in a democratic state?
3. What are the fundamental rights protected by the Constitution?
4. What does the constitutional review of laws consist of?
5. What is the role of the head of state in a presidential regime?
6. What are the differences between direct and representative democracy?
7. How can a citizen challenge an unconstitutional law?
8. What are the limits of the powers of a President of the Republic?
9. How does the appeal to the Constitutional Court work?
10. What are the issues at stake in constitutional revisions?

2. Criminal Law and Criminal Procedure

11. What is the difference between a traffic

ticket, a misdemeanor and a crime?

12. What are the constituent elements of a criminal offence?

13. What are the stages of criminal proceedings?

14. What are the rights of a suspect when arrested?

15. What is the presumption of innocence?

16. What are the criteria for parole?

17. How does police custody work and what are its legal limits?

18. What is the difference between a custodial sentence and an alternative sentence?

19. What are the means of defense in criminal law?

20. How does a trial before an Assize Court work?

3. Civil Law and Obligations

21. What are the fundamental principles of contract law?

22. What is the difference between civil and criminal liability?

23. How to prove the existence of a contract in court?

24. What are the rights and duties of spouses in matrimonial law?

25. How does legal succession work in the event of death without a will?

26. What are the conditions for the validity of a contract?

27. How to contest an acknowledgement of debt?

28. What are the remedies in the event of hidden defects in a property sold?

29. How to cancel a contract due to fraud or error?

30. What are the limitation periods in civil matters?

4. Labor Law and Social Protection

31. What are the fundamental rights of workers?

32. How does a dismissal procedure take place?

33. What are the remedies in the event of harassment at work?

34. What does the mutual termination of an employment contract consist of?

35. What are the employer's obligations regarding safety?

36. What are the different types of employment contracts?

37. How does the right to strike work?

38. What are the criteria for discrimination at

work?

39. How does the paid leave system work?

40. What are the rights of a self-employed person when faced with a defaulting client?

5. Business and Corporate Law

41. What are the steps in creating a business in law?

42. How does the liability of the company director work?

43. What are the essential clauses of a commercial contract?

44. What is unfair competition in business law?

45. How does a receivership procedure work?

46. What are the different legal statuses of a company?

47. How to legally protect a trademark?

48. What is corporate law?

49. What are the possible remedies in the event of a commercial dispute?

50. What are the legal obligations regarding invoicing?

6. Environmental Law and Urban Planning

51. What are the main environmental

protection laws?

52. How does water and energy law work?

53. What are citizens' rights in the face of industrial pollution?

54. How does the building permit work?

55. What are the remedies in the event of non-compliance with planning law?

56. What are the penalties for environmental damage?

57. How should companies comply with green standards?

58. What are the principles of sustainable development in law?

59. What are the obligations of States in the area of climate change?

60. How to protect a classified natural area?

7. Digital Law and Data Protection

61. What are the GDPR obligations for businesses?

62. How to legally protect a website against plagiarism?

63. What are a user's rights over their personal data?

64. What are the penalties for cybercrime?

65. How can an individual delete their personal data from the internet?

66. What are the legal obligations of influencers on social networks?

67. How to prove cyber harassment in court?

68. What are the remedies in the event of online identity theft?

69. What are the intellectual property rules on YouTube?

70. How to legally protect a mobile application?

8. National Security and International Law

71. What are the principles of international humanitarian law?

72. How can a country declare a state of emergency?

73. What are the obligations of States in the fight against terrorism?

74. What are the limits of the right of humanitarian intervention?

75. How does extradition work between two countries?

76. What are the rights of prisoners of war under the Geneva Convention?

77. What are the criteria for granting political asylum?

78. How does the International Criminal Court (ICC) work?

79. What are the UN's missions in global security?

80. What are the remedies in the event of a violation of human rights?

9. Private and Public Security Law

81. What are the powers of a private security agent?

82. What are the conditions for carrying a weapon on duty?

83. How does video surveillance work in business?

84. What are the obligations of private security companies?

85. What are the rights and limits of law enforcement in matters of arrest?

86. How does the right to self-defense work?

87. What are the rules governing the use of drones for surveillance?

88. What are the remedies in the event of police violence?

89. How does Cybersecurity work in the banking sector?

90. What are the penalties for bank fraud?

10. Insurance Law

91. What are the obligations of an insurer towards its customers?

92. How does liability insurance work?

93. What are the steps to report a claim?

94. What are the time limits for obtaining compensation after an accident?

95. How to contest an insurance refusal of compensation?

96. What is insurance fraud and what are the penalties?

97. What are the insured's obligations in the event of bodily injury?

98. How does life insurance work in the event of the death of the insured?

99. What are the differences between compulsory and optional insurance?

100. What are the remedies in the event of a dispute with an insurance company?

11. Family Law

101. What are the conditions for obtaining a divorce?

102. How does shared child custody work after divorce?

103. What are the rights of an unmarried father over his child?

104.   How does an adoption take place in France?

105.   What are the rights and duties of grandparents towards their grandchildren?

106.   How does alimony work and how is it calculated?

107.   What are the conditions for legally changing your last name?

108.   What are the remedies in cases of domestic violence?

109.   How does family mediation work?

110.   What are the rights of a child born out of wedlock?

12. Consumer Law

111.   What are the consumer's rights in the event of a defective product?

112.   How to exercise your right of withdrawal after an online purchase?

113.   What are companies' obligations regarding false advertising?

114.   How to file a complaint against a company for abusive practices?

115.   What are the remedies in the event of over-indebtedness?

116.   How to report an internet scam?

117.   What does the legal guarantee of conformity of a product consist of?

118.   What are the consumer's rights in the event of a service provider going bankrupt?

119.   What are banks' obligations regarding customer protection?

120.   How to get a refund for a fraudulent purchase on a bank card?

13. Intellectual Property Law

121.   How to protect an artistic work against plagiarism?

122.   What are the copyrights on a self-published book?

123.   What does filing a patent involve and how do I obtain one?

124.   How does logo and brand protection work?

125.   What are the remedies in the event of intellectual property infringement?

126.   How long does copyright protection last?

127.   How to prove the seniority of an artistic creation?

128.   What is fair use in copyright?

129.   How to register an invention with the INPI?

130.   What are the legal risks of illegally sharing movies online?

14. Digital Security and Cybercrime

131.   What are the main cybersecurity threats?

132.   How does phishing work and how to protect yourself from it?

133.   What are a user's rights in the event of an account hack?

134.   What are the penalties for hacking a computer system?

135.   How to protect a company against computer attacks?

136.   What is the right to digital oblivion?

137.   How does online identity theft work?

138.   What are the remedies in the event of defamation on the internet?

139.   How to report a fraudulent site to the authorities?

140.   What are the obligations of social networks regarding user protection?

15. Maritime and Air Law

141.   What are passengers' rights in the event of a flight cancellation?

142.   How does airline liability work in the event of an accident?

143.   What is international maritime law?

144.   What are the remedies in the event of loss of baggage by an airline?

145.   How does ship pollution regulation work?

146.   What are the rights of seafarers in terms of labor law?

147.   How does maritime piracy law work?

148.   What documents are required to legally navigate the high seas?

149.   How do states control air transport?

150.   What are the airlines' obligations in the event of overbooking?

16. Health Law and Bioethics

151.   What are patients' rights in the face of medical errors?

152.   What is informed consent in

medicine?

153. What are the remedies in the event of medical malpractice?

154. How does the law on end of life and euthanasia work?

155. What are hospitals' obligations regarding the protection of medical data?

156. How does organ donation legislation work?

157. What are the legal conditions for carrying out clinical trials?

158. How does the protection of disabled people work in law?

159. What are the legal limits of telemedicine?

160. What are the rights of patients with rare diseases?

17. Public and Private International Law

161. How does extradition work between countries?

162. What does state sovereignty consist of in international law?

163. What are the mechanisms for settling international conflicts?

164. How does international

marriage recognition work?

165.   What are the rights of refugees under the Geneva Convention?

166.   How does diplomatic law and ambassadorial immunity work?

167.   What are the criteria for a State to be recognized by the international community?

168.   How are international treaties applied in national law?

169.   What are the rights of expatriate workers?

170.   How to resolve a commercial dispute between companies from different countries?

18. Rural and Environmental Law

171.   What are the legal obligations of farmers regarding the environment?

172.   What is land law and agricultural land protection?

173.   What are consumers' rights regarding GMOs?

174.   How does pesticide use legislation work?

175.   What are the obligations of companies regarding waste management?

176.   How to legally protect a

threatened ecosystem?

177.   What are the penalties for illegal logging?

178.   How do states regulate industrial fishing?

179.   What does ecological compensation consist of in environmental law?

180.   How do international standards influence environmental law?

19. Security and Terrorism

181.   What are the legal means to combat terrorism?

182.   How does security communications monitoring work?

183.   What are the laws governing the use of drones for national security?

184.   How does the freezing of terrorist organizations' assets work?

185.   What recourse do citizens have in the face of abusive surveillance measures?

186.   What is the fight against money laundering in the financing of terrorism?

187.   How should law enforcement handle terrorist crises?

188.   What are the obligations

of digital platforms to combat terrorist propaganda?

189.   How to protect a country's critical infrastructure?

190.   What are the impacts of international law on the fight against terrorism?

20. Law and Ethics in Artificial Intelligence

191.   What are the legal issues of artificial intelligence in terms of data protection?

192.   How to legally regulate the use of algorithms in public decision-making?

193.   What are citizens' rights regarding automated decisions by companies?

194.   What is the legal liability of AI creators?

195.   What are the ethical challenges associated with autonomous weapons and military AI?

196.   How to protect works created by artificial intelligence in terms of copyright?

197.   What are the obligations of companies developing chatbots and

virtual assistants?

198. How is AI used in crime prevention and what are the legal limits?

199. What are the principles of European law regarding the regulation of AI?

200. How can governments regulate the responsible development of AI?

CHAPTER 11.ART AND ENTERTAINMENT

Introduction: Artificial Intelligence in the Service of Art and Entertainment

Artificial intelligence is transforming the world of **art and entertainment** , opening the way to new forms of creativity. Thanks to AI, artists, creators and developers have powerful tools to **generate music, write screenplays, animate films and design immersive video games** .

Far from replacing human creativity, AI acts as a **catalyst** , allowing us to explore new aesthetics, accelerate the creative process and push the boundaries of artistic innovation. From composers to filmmakers, writers and game designers, everyone can leverage this technology to enrich their works and offer unique experiences to the audience.

In this collection of **prompts dedicated to art and entertainment** , we will explore several key applications of AI:

- **AI-generated music (AIVA, OpenAI Jukebox)** : AI composes original tracks, adapts musical styles and assists musicians in creating unique soundtracks.

- **Automated storytelling and scenario creation** : AI algorithms help write compelling stories, generate realistic dialogues, and structure engaging narratives.

- **Optimized animation and special effects** : Thanks to AI, animation becomes more fluid and realistic, while visual effects reach a new level of precision.

- **Video games with adaptive AI** : AI makes it possible to design games where characters and environments dynamically adapt to players' actions, thus providing a more immersive experience.

- **Interactive experiences and augmented realities** : AI is revolutionizing forms of entertainment by enabling unique interactive experiences, from immersive cinema to augmented reality art installations.

With these advances, we are witnessing a **new era of creativity** , where the boundaries between man and machine are blurring to give birth to ever more daring works. **This prompts guide will allow you to explore and exploit the full potential of AI in art and entertainment.**

Here are 200 prompts in the field of Art and Entertainment , divided into different categories:

1. Artistic Creation and Painting

1. Describe a futuristic work of art inspired by artificial intelligence.
2. Imagine a painting that represents the fusion between nature and technology.
3. What would be the style of a 21st century painter influenced by digital technology?
4. How to represent time in painting in an original way?
5. Describe a mural that tells an inspiring story.
6. What would be the portrait of a legendary character revisited in cyberpunk style?
7. Imagine a surrealist work that explores dreams and the unconscious.
8. What symbols should be used to represent rebirth and renewal in art?
9. Describe a painting where colors and shapes give an impression of movement.
10. Imagine a minimalist painting that evokes solitude and reflection.

2. Music and Sound Composition

11. Create lyrics for a song about escape and freedom.
12. How to compose a melody that evokes nostalgia for a past moment?

13. Imagine a piece of electronic music inspired by the sounds of nature.

14. Describe a perfect soundtrack for a science fiction movie.

15. How to transcribe a strong emotion through a musical composition?

16. Which instruments should you choose for a mysterious and immersive atmosphere?

17. Imagine a concept album inspired by the four elements: water, earth, air, fire.

18. How to integrate sounds from everyday life into a musical work?

19. Describe the ideal music to accompany a seaside sunset.

20. Imagine a collaboration between two artists of opposing styles.

3. Cinema and Audiovisual

21. Write a synopsis for a dystopian movie about a world dominated by AI.

22. Describe a movie scene where time stands still.

23. Imagine a new ending for a famous movie.

24. What key elements make a film a cinematic masterpiece?

25. Describe a science fiction setting that seems believable and immersive.

26. How to make a movie character unforgettable through design?

27. Imagine a choreographed fight scene with an artistic touch.

28. What are the essential elements of a good horror movie?

29. How to film an intense emotional scene in an original way?

30. Describe an intriguing trailer for an adventure film.

4. Literature and Creative Writing

31. Imagine the beginning of a fantasy novel inspired by ancient myths.

32. Describe a character whose story takes place in a post-apocalyptic world.

33. How to write a powerful dialogue between two characters in conflict?

34. Create a poem that evokes melancholy and the passing of time.

35. What are the elements of a good plot twist in storytelling?

36. Imagine a love letter written in the distant future.

37. Describe a fantasy world where music has magical powers.

38. What are the ingredients of a good detective

novel?

39. How to transcribe the deep thoughts of a character in a few lines?

40. Imagine a children's story that teaches a beautiful life lesson.

5. Photography and Visual Art

41. What are the essential elements of a successful photographic composition?

42. Describe the perfect photograph to capture a moment of pure joy.

43. How to use natural light to create a dramatic effect in a photo?

44. What are the advantages of black and white in photographic art?

45. Imagine a series of photos that tell a story without words.

46. How to express loneliness through an image?

47. What are the best subjects for a macro photo?

48. Describe a photograph that captures an important historical moment.

49. What shooting angles give an impression of grandeur?

50. How to photograph a street scene that conveys a strong emotion?

6. Video Games and Animation

51. Describe the concept of a video game based on players' dreams.

52. How to design an iconic video game character?

53. What are the key elements of good artistic direction in video games?

54. Imagine a role-playing game where decisions profoundly influence the story.

55. How to create an immersive atmosphere through game music?

56. Describe a video game setting inspired by an underwater world.

57. What animation styles work best for a narrative game?

58. How do you make a video game enemy terrifying and memorable?

59. Imagine an educational game that teaches a skill in a fun way.

60. What are the best ways to incorporate artistic elements into an action game?

7. Fashion and Design

61. Describe a clothing collection inspired by wilderness.

62. How to integrate artificial intelligence into

fashion design?

63. Imagine a futuristic outfit that adapts to the emotions of the wearer.

64. What are the essential elements of a memorable logo?

65. Describe a gala dress inspired by Greek mythology.

66. How to design an outfit that combines comfort and elegance?

67. Imagine a shoe design inspired by the elements of the earth.

68. How to integrate sustainability into contemporary fashion?

69. Describe a piece of haute couture with a unique concept.

70. What patterns and colors work best to express modernity?

8. Performing Arts and Performance

71. Imagine a theatrical performance without dialogue, based only on movements.

72. How to captivate an audience from the first seconds of a show?

73. Describe a modern ballet inspired by the city and its rhythms.

74. What are the challenges of staging a contemporary opera?

75. How to use light to bring a performance scene to life?

76. Describe an innovative circus show that combines tradition and new technologies.

77. How to make a play interactive with the audience?

78. What are the key elements of good stand-up comedy?

79. Describe an outdoor artistic performance that draws crowds.

80. How can the performing arts raise awareness for a social cause?

9. Pop Culture and Media

81. How to analyze the cultural impact of a cult TV series?

82. What are the ingredients of a good musical parody?

83. Describe an iconic scene from an alternate version movie.

84. What are the effects of social media on artistic creation?

85. Imagine an unlikely mashup between two famous franchises.

86. How do internet memes influence contemporary culture?

87. Describe an arts festival that showcases

emerging talent.

88. What are the secrets of the virality of an artistic work?

89. How are influencers redefining art and fashion?

90. Describe an interactive art exhibit for a digital museum.

10. Comics and Illustration

91. Imagine a superhero whose power is tied to human emotions.

92. Describe a futuristic city in steampunk style for a comic book.

93. How to transcribe an intense action scene into an illustration?

94. What are the elements of a good comic book layout?

95. Describe a charismatic villain for a science fiction manga.

96. Imagine a comic book without dialogue that tells a poignant story.

97. What graphic styles are best suited for a humorous webcomic?

98. How to play with colors to enhance the atmosphere of a comic book?

99. Describe a fantasy hero with an original and striking appearance.

100. How to illustrate a dream scene in dreamlike style?

11. Architecture and Space Design

101. Imagine a building inspired by the organic forms of nature.

102. How to create architecture that combines tradition and modernity?

103. Describe a house of the future using innovative materials.

104. What elements make an art space immersive?

105. How to design an interactive museum for a new generation?

106. Describe a place that fuses art, nature and technology.

107. Imagine a city where every neighborhood has a different artistic style.

108. What are the principles of good interior design inspired by minimalism?

109. Describe a concert hall designed for perfect acoustics.

110. How to integrate artificial intelligence into architectural design?

12. Immersive Experiences and Digital Art

111.   Imagine an augmented reality artwork that interacts with viewers.

112.   What are the essential elements of a good digital art project?

113.   Describe an immersive experience where light and sound are the protagonists.

114.   How to combine artificial intelligence and artistic creativity?

115.   Imagine an art installation where the visitors' emotions influence the work.

116.   What are the challenges of artistic creation in the metaverse?

117.   Describe a generative work that evolves over time.

118.   How to tell a story only through holograms?

119.   Imagine an interactive art exhibition in an urban space.

120.   What are the impacts of AI on digital image creation?

13. Calligraphy and Typography

121.   Imagine a new typeface inspired by nature.

122.   What are the principles of good calligraphy composition?

123.   Describe a logo designed exclusively with artistic typography.

124.   How to modernize the traditional art of calligraphy in contemporary design?

125.   Imagine a font that changes with the time of day.

126.   What are the key elements of expressive typography?

127.   Describe a project where typography becomes an artistic work in its own right.

128.   How to use letters to tell a visual story?

129.   Imagine a movie poster that relies solely on typographic work.

130.   What are the challenges of designing a legible and artistic font?

14. Culture and History of Art

131.   What are the artistic movements that most influence contemporary culture?

132.   Describe a little-known work that deserves to be rediscovered.

133.   How has street art evolved over the decades?

134.   Who are the modern artists who

push the boundaries of creativity?

135.   Imagine an exhibition that traces the evolution of digital art.

136.   How could a painting from the past be revisited in a modern style?

137.   What are the links between fashion and art history?

138.   Describe a museum of the future where each work reacts to visitors.

139.   How to integrate ancient techniques into contemporary art?

140.   Which artists revolutionized their era with their audacity?

15. Performance and Street Art

141.   Describe an artistic performance that makes passers-by react in the street.

142.   What are the elements of a captivating street performance?

143.   Imagine an interactive statue that changes with the seasons.

144.   How to mix theater and visual art in the same performance?

145.   Describe a dance inspired by the movements of nature.

146.   What are the challenges of live art in public spaces?

147.   Imagine an urban fresco that evolves over time.

148.   How to transform a neighborhood into an open-air art gallery?

149.   Describe an art installation that raises awareness for a social cause.

150.   What are the elements of good staging for an outdoor show?

16. Multi-sensory experiences

151.   Imagine an artistic event that appeals to visitors' five senses.

152.   What are some ways to integrate smell into an immersive experience?

153.   Describe an installation where touch plays a central role.

154.   How to combine music and painting in the same artistic experience?

155.   Imagine a gallery where each work generates a unique sound when approached.

156.   What are the challenges of creating a sensory experience in art?

157.   Describe a work where water and light create a captivating effect.

158.   How can artificial intelligence be used to personalize an artistic experience?

159.   Imagine an installation where the viewer himself becomes the work of art.

160.   What are the elements of a successful immersive show?

17. Art and Artificial Intelligence

161.   How can AI help create new art forms?

162.   Describe a work of art generated entirely by AI.

163.   What are the ethical dilemmas related to the use of AI in art?

164.   Imagine a robot that can paint by imitating different artistic styles.

165.   How can AI collaborate with human artists?

166.   What are the risks of standardization in AI-generated art?

167.   Describe an art project that fuses deep learning and human creativity.

168.   How can AI analyze and interpret classical works of art?

169.   Imagine a digital gallery where each painting is generated in real time.

170.   What are the possible futures of AI-assisted art?

18. Art and Social Commitment

171.	How can art raise awareness of environmental issues?

172.	Describe a work that denounces social injustice.

173.	What are the best examples of committed art throughout history?

174.	Imagine a mural that tells the story of a community.

175.	How can art be a tool for emotional healing?

176.	Describe an artistic performance that brings together different cultures.

177.	Which contemporary artists use their art to convey a message?

178.	Imagine an exhibition about cultural diversity around the world.

179.	How can cinema influence mentalities on a social issue?

180.	Describe an artistic initiative that helps people in difficulty.

19. Art and Innovation

181.	How are NFTs transforming the art market?

182. Imagine a work that can only be seen in virtual reality.

183. What are the new materials used in contemporary art?

184. Describe a concept for a mobile, interactive art gallery.

185. How can art merge with science to create new experiences?

186. Imagine a city where architecture is designed like an immense work of art.

187. What are the challenges of digital art compared to traditional art?

188. How to use biotechnology to create living art?

189. Describe a sculpture that interacts with its environment.

190. What are the possible futures of art in the digital age?

20. Art and Experimentation

191. Imagine an exhibition where visitors have to create the final work themselves.

192. How to integrate recycled materials into an artistic installation?

193. Describe a painting that changes appearance depending on the

temperature.

194.   What are the challenges of kinetic art and movement in sculpture?

195.   Imagine an artistic performance where music and dance merge with technology.

196.   How to use light to create artistic optical illusions?

197.   Describe a work that explores the relationship between humans and artificial intelligence.

198.   What are the key concepts for creating a participatory art installation?

199.   Imagine a festival where each spectator becomes an actor in a work in real time.

200.   How can art push the boundaries of human perception?

LIST OF ARTIFICIAL INTELLIGENCE PLATFORMS BY CATEGORY

Artificial intelligence is now used in many fields thanks to specialized platforms. Here is a classification of the main AI platforms by category:

1. Text Generation and Natural Language Processing (NLP)

- **ChatGPT** (OpenAI) – Text generation and conversational assistant
- **Claude** (Anthropic) – Advanced Natural Language AI Assistant
- **Bard** (Google AI) – Chatbot and Text Generation
- **Jasper AI** – Marketing and SEO Content Writing
- **Copy.ai** – Advertising copy and text generation
- **Writesonic** – Writing content optimized for the web
- **Hugging Face** – Open-source library for NLP and language models
- **DeepL Write** – Text enhancement and correction

2. Image and Video Generation

- **DALL·E** (OpenAI) – Generate images from text
- **Stable Diffusion** – Open-source AI image creation
- **Midjourney** – Generation of artistic and realistic illustrations
- **Runway ML** – AI-powered video generation and editing
- **Deep Dream Generator** – AI Image Transformation
- **DeepArt** – AI-powered artistic image creation
- **Pika Labs** – AI Image Animation and Video Creation

3. Voice Generation and Speech Synthesis

- **ElevenLabs** – Realistic and personalized speech synthesis
- **Descript** – Audio/Video Editing and Voice Cloning
- **Murf AI** – Natural Voice Generation for Videos and Podcasts
- **Resemble AI** – Voice Cloning & Custom Synthetic Voices
- **Google Text-to-Speech** – Advanced Text-to-Speech
- **Amazon Polly** – Text to Natural Speech Conversion

- **IBM Watson Text to Speech** – AI Text-to-Speech

---

4. Coding and Software Development

- **GitHub Copilot** – AI-Assisted Code Generation
- **Codeium** – Open-source AI coding assistant
- **Tabnine** – AI-powered autocompletion and code suggestions
- **Amazon CodeWhisperer** – Coding Assistance for Developers
- **DeepCode** – Detection and correction of errors in code
- **PolyCoder** – Open-source AI-powered code generation

---

5. Cybersecurity and Threat Detection

- **Darktrace** – Cyberattack detection and response
- **CrowdStrike Falcon** – Endpoint Threat Protection
- **Microsoft Defender AI** – Advanced AI-powered security and protection
- **SentinelOne** – Intrusion Detection and Prevention with AI
- **IBM Watson for Cyber Security** – Cyber threat analysis

---

6. Finance and Economics

- **Kavout** – Analysis and forecast of financial markets
- **AlphaSense** – Automated Financial Research and Analysis
- **ZestFinance** – Credit Scoring and Risk Management
- **Numerai** – AI-based financial market modeling
- **Kensho (S&P Global)** – Economic Data Analysis with AI

7. Education and Training

- **Socratic by Google** – Homework Help and Concept Explanation
- **Quizlet AI** – Generation of interactive quizzes and exercises
- **Grammarly** – AI-powered text correction and enhancement
- **ScribeSense** – Automated Handwritten Copy Assessment
- **Querium** – Virtual Tutor for Science and Math

8. Health and Medicine

- **IBM Watson Health** – Medical Data Analysis and Diagnostics

- **Qure.ai** – Medical image interpretation (radiology, MRI)
- **Viz.ai** – Early Stroke Detection Using AI
- **Paige AI** – Biopsy Analysis and Cancer Detection
- **Aidoc** – Assistance to radiologists for the analysis of medical images

9. Marketing and E-Commerce

- **Persado** – Creating AI-powered marketing campaigns
- **Phrasee** – AI Email & Ad Optimization
- **Adzooma** – Automated management of advertising campaigns
- **Dynamic Yield** – Personalization of product recommendations
- **Salesforce Einstein** – Marketing Analytics and Predictions

10. Industry and Automation

- **Siemens MindSphere** – Industrial analysis and optimization with AI
- **Uptake** – Predictive maintenance of industrial equipment
- **SparkCognition** – AI for Industrial Operations Management
- **Falkonry** – Monitoring and detection of anomalies in production

- **Vention** – Automation of industrial processes with AI

11. Transport and Mobility

- **Tesla Autopilot** – Self-driving and driver assistance
- **Waymo AI** – Autonomous Vehicles and Traffic Management
- **Nuro AI** – Autonomous delivery by AI vehicles
- **HERE Technologies** – Navigation systems and traffic optimization
- **Zoox** – Robotaxis and smart urban mobility

12. Agriculture and Environment

- **Taranis** – Crop monitoring and disease detection
- **FarmLogs** – Optimizing agricultural yields with AI
- **Blue River Technology** – Precision Agriculture and Smart Spraying
- **The Climate Corporation** – Weather Prediction for Agriculture
- **Civis Analytics** – Environmental Resource Management

13. Law and Security

- **ROSS Intelligence** – Legal research and text

analysis

- **Casetext CARA AI** – Assistance to lawyers for case analysis
- **PredPol** – Crime Prediction and Risk Management
- **Clearview AI** – Facial Recognition and Identification
- **ComplyAdvantage** – Fraud Detection and Regulatory Compliance

14. Art and Entertainment

- **AIVA** – AI-assisted music composition
- **OpenAI Jukebox** – Generate Music from Text
- **Runway ML** – AI Animation and Special Effects
- **Scenario AI** – Generation of graphics and assets for video games
- **Deep Dream Generator** – Artistic Image Transformation with AI

CONCLUSION: ARTIFICIAL INTELLIGENCE, A UNIVERSE OF INFINITE POSSIBILITIES

Artificial intelligence is more than just a technology: it's a revolution that's redefining the way we work, innovate, and create. Through these **2,200 prompts** , we explored **the many applications of AI** , spanning fields as diverse as medicine, finance, education, content creation, industry, and more.

This book has provided you with **a wide range of ideas and inspirations** to harness the power of AI in your professional and personal projects. Whether you are an entrepreneur looking to automate your business, a developer wanting to improve your algorithms, a creative exploring new forms of expression, or a researcher looking for innovation, AI offers **unprecedented opportunities** .

Towards an AI-Assisted Future

The rapid evolution of artificial intelligence means that **today's possibilities are just the beginning** . Every day, new advances emerge, making AI **more powerful, accessible, and integrated into our lives** . This book is not meant to be an end in itself, but **a starting point** to help you **experiment, create, and push the boundaries** of what's possible with AI.

Whether you use these prompts to **optimize your processes, generate content, automate tasks or**

develop new ideas , remember that **AI is a tool for creativity and innovation** . Those who can use it intelligently will be the leaders of tomorrow.

The future belongs to those who dare to experiment with artificial intelligence. It's your turn!

www.ingramcontent.com/pod-product-compliance
Lightning Source LLC
LaVergne TN
LVHW051733050326
832903LV00023B/902